A Day To Remember

David & Debbie's Wedding

Debbie Wu & David Chang

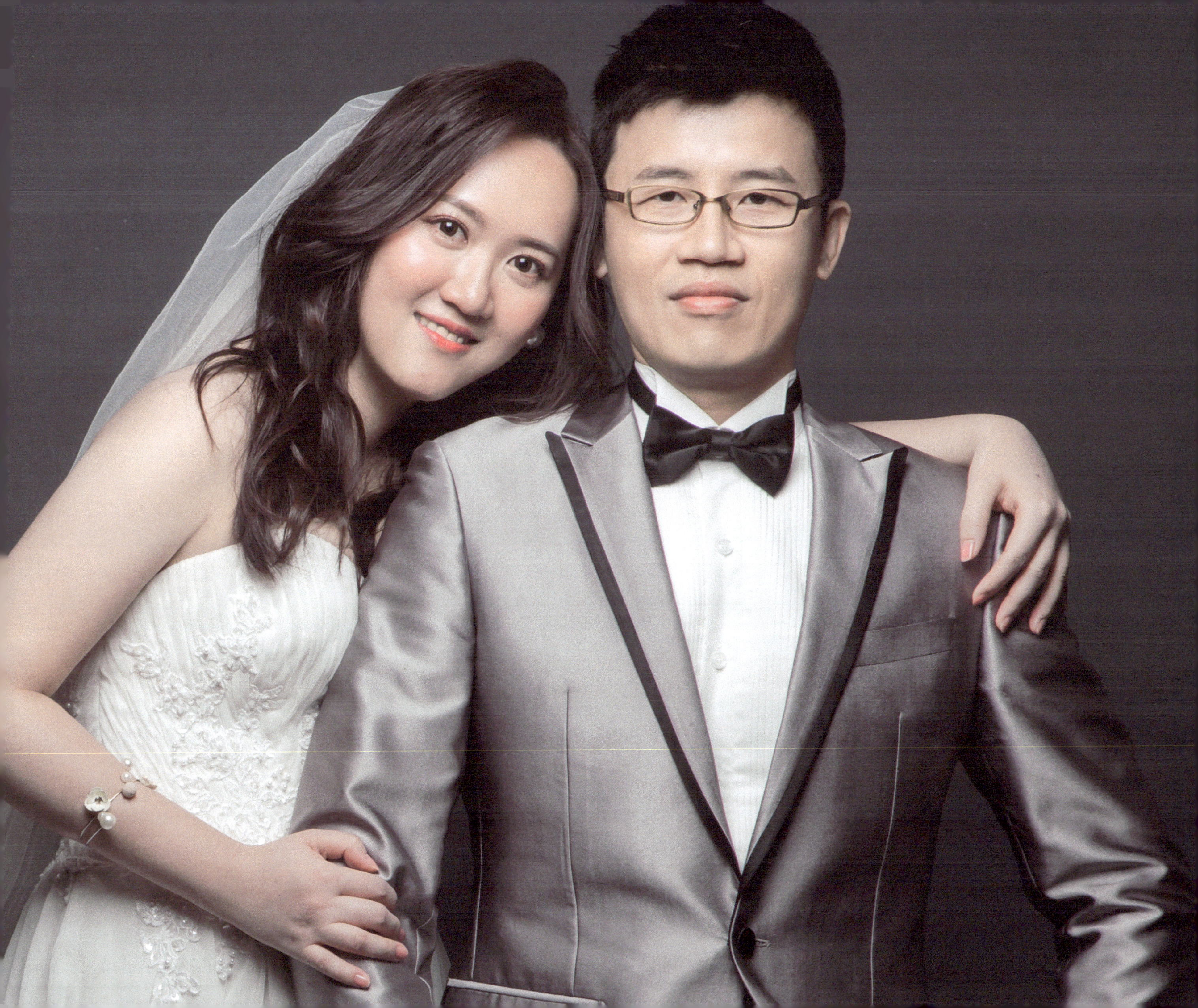

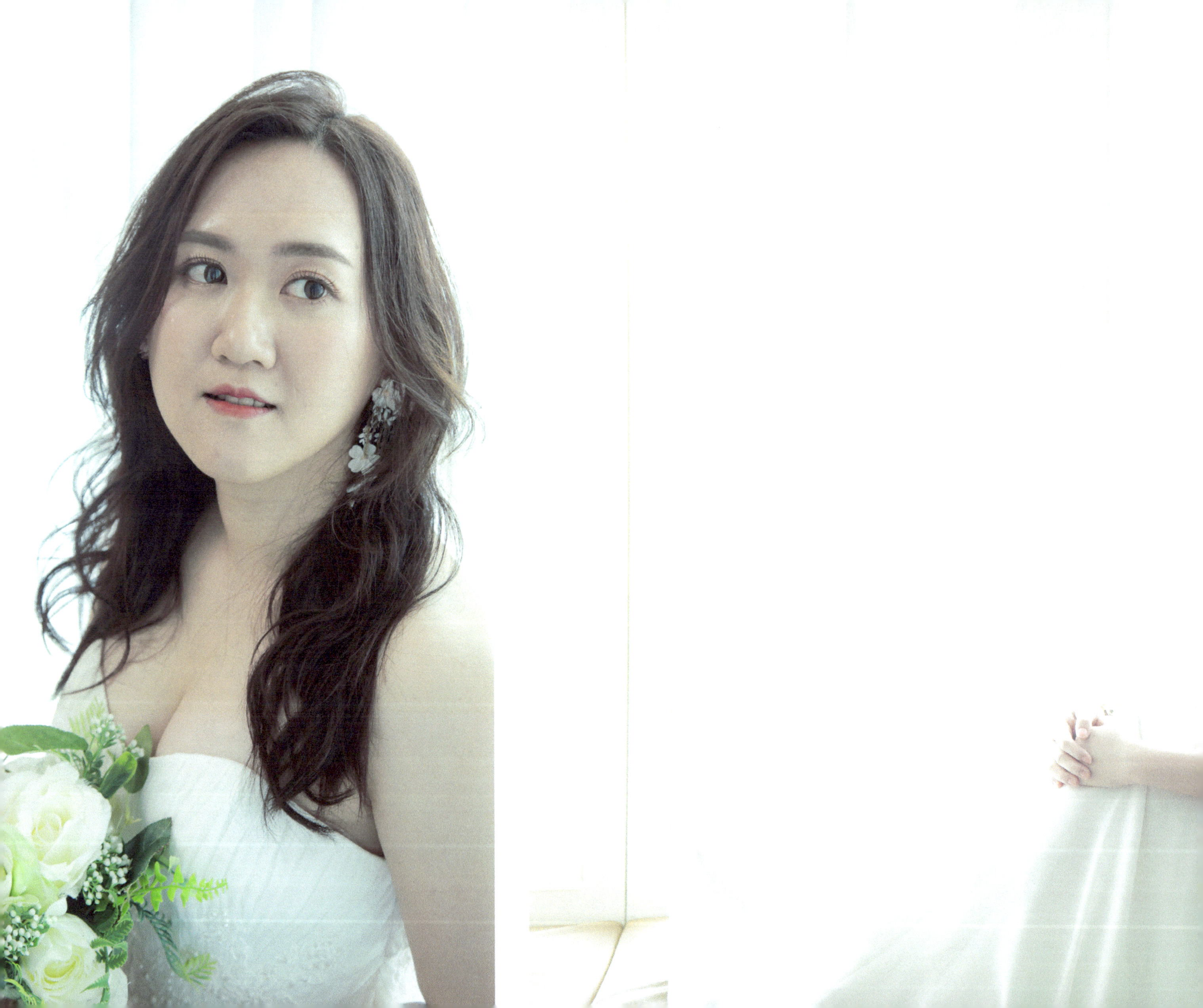

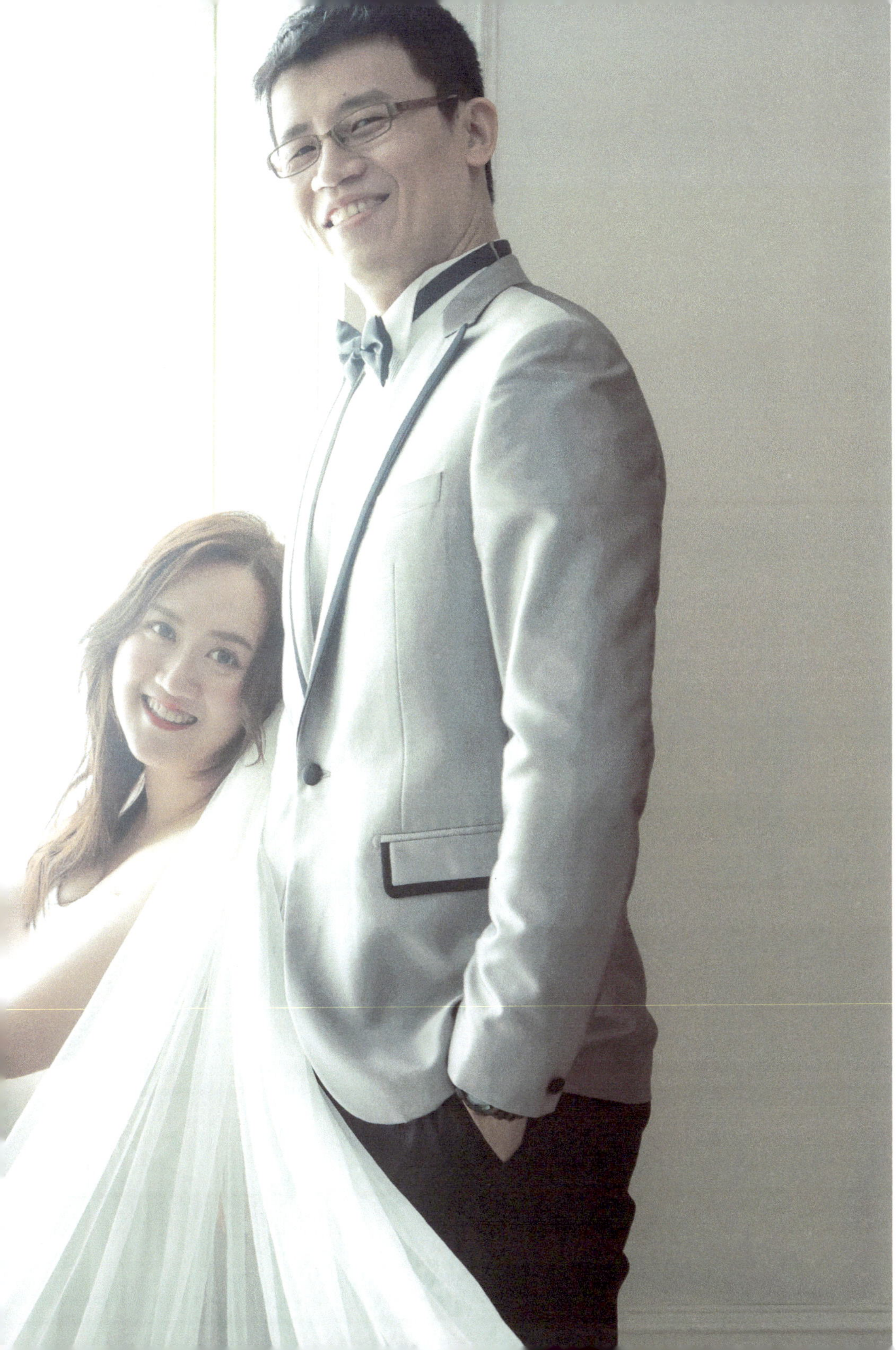
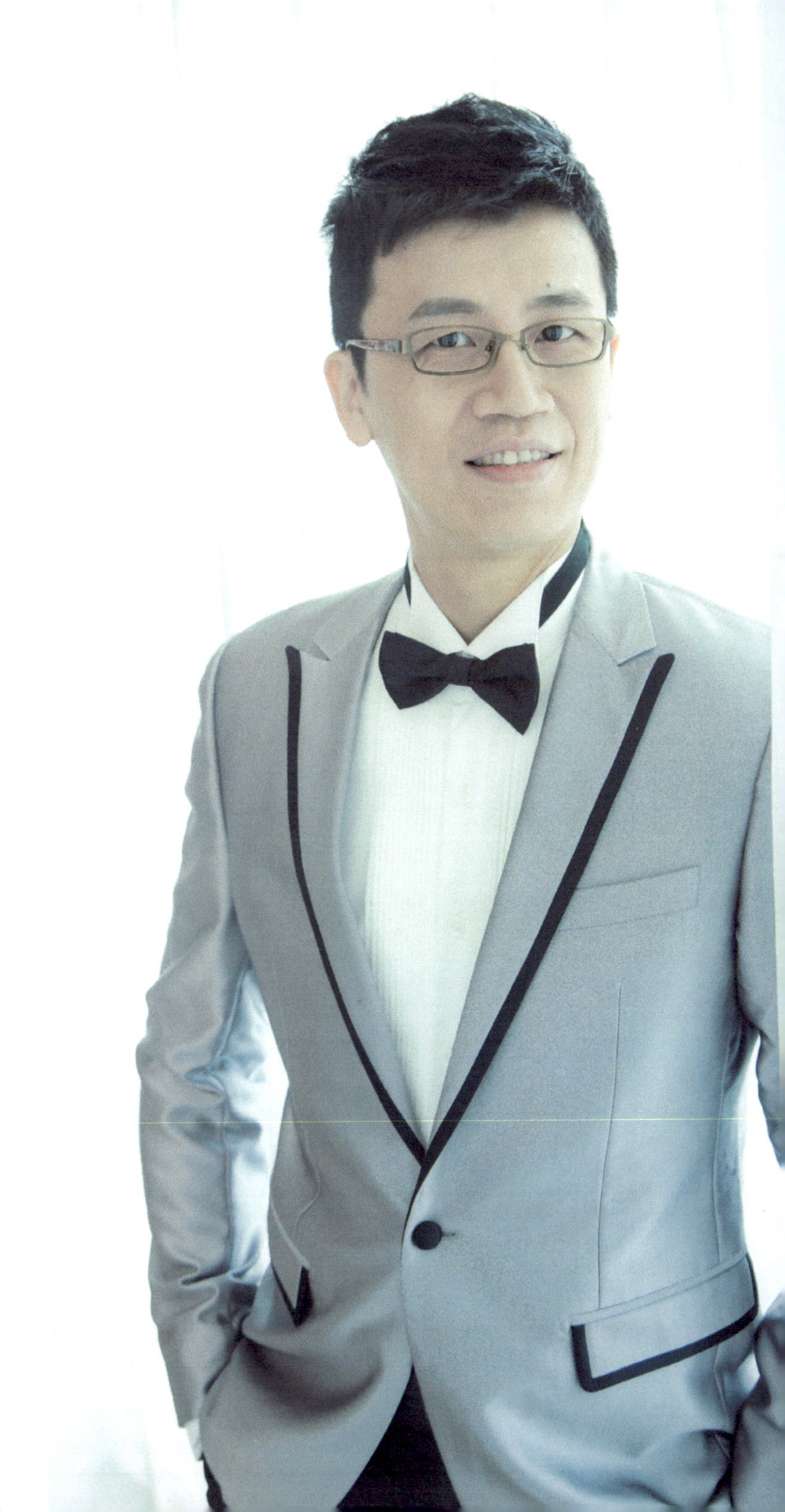

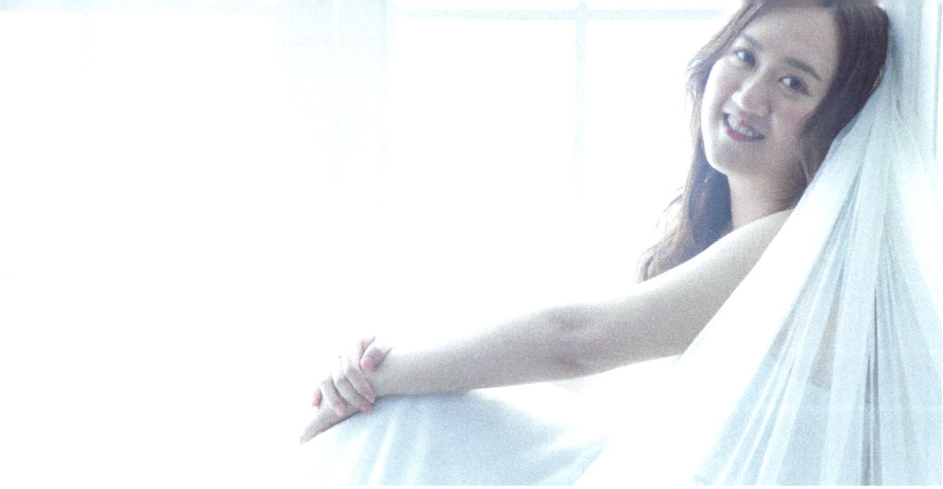
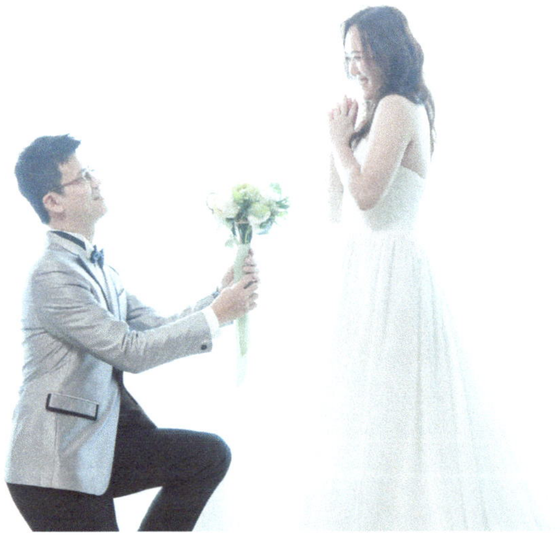
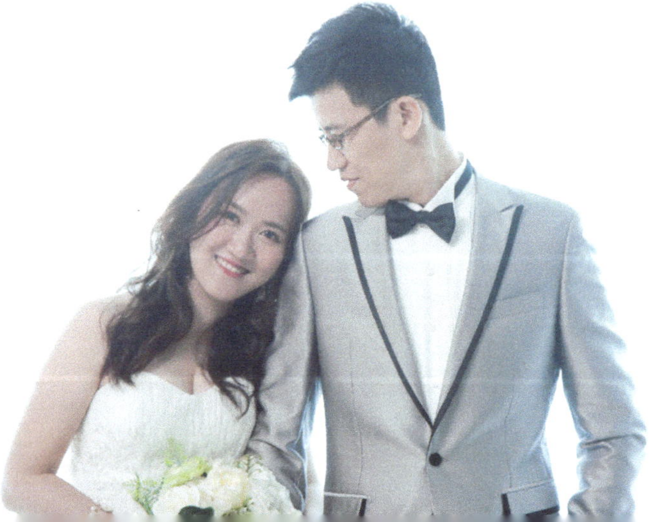

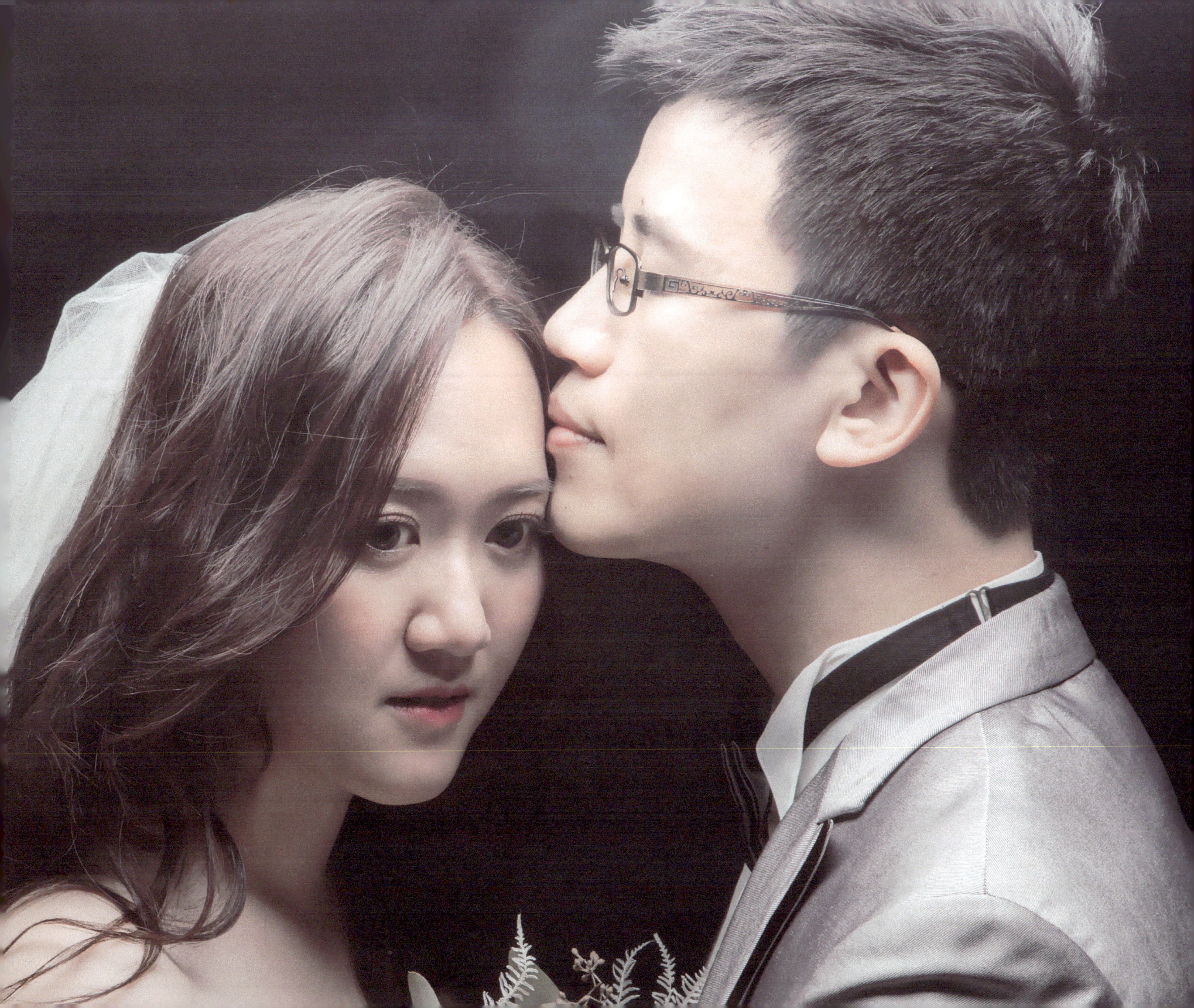

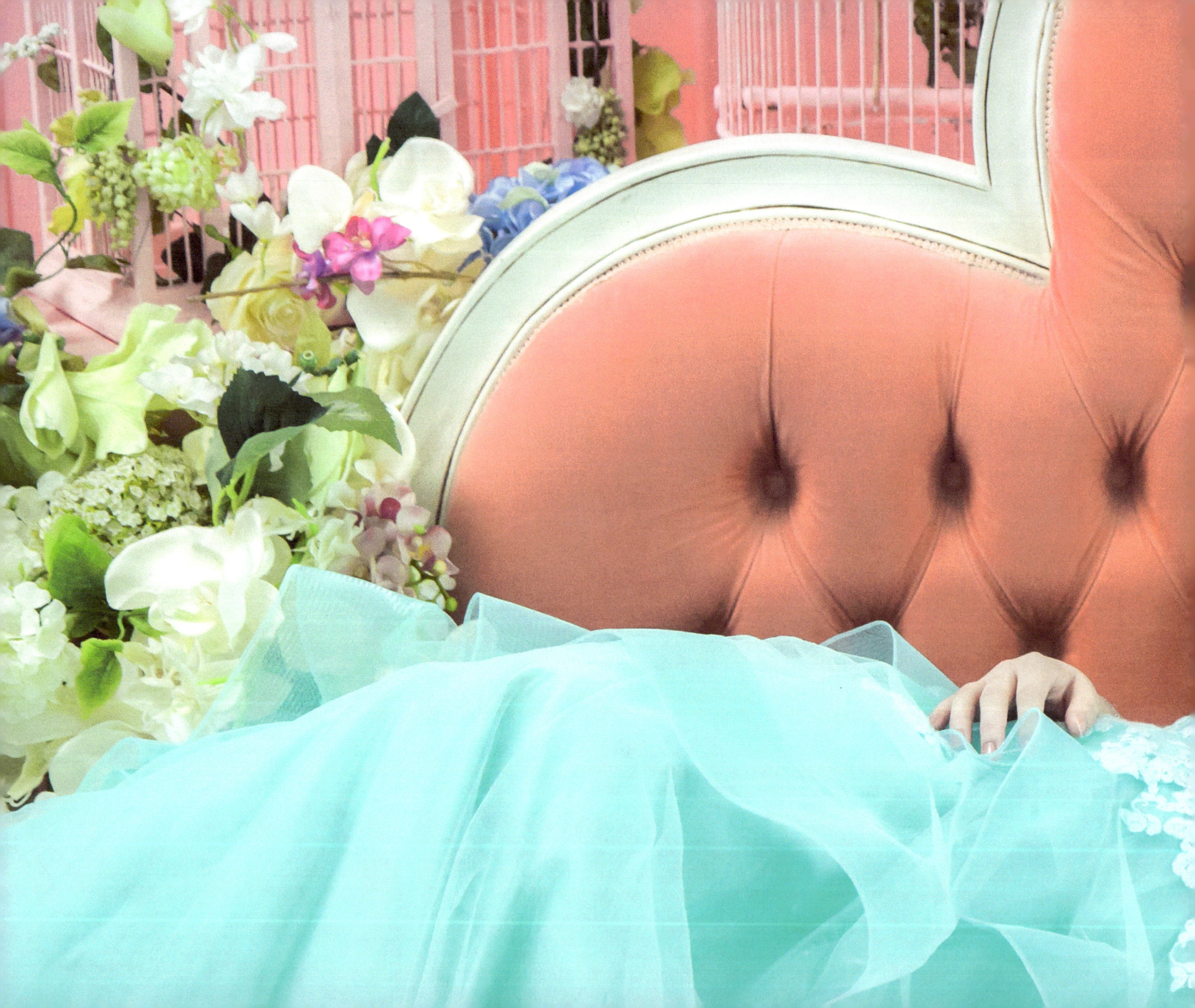

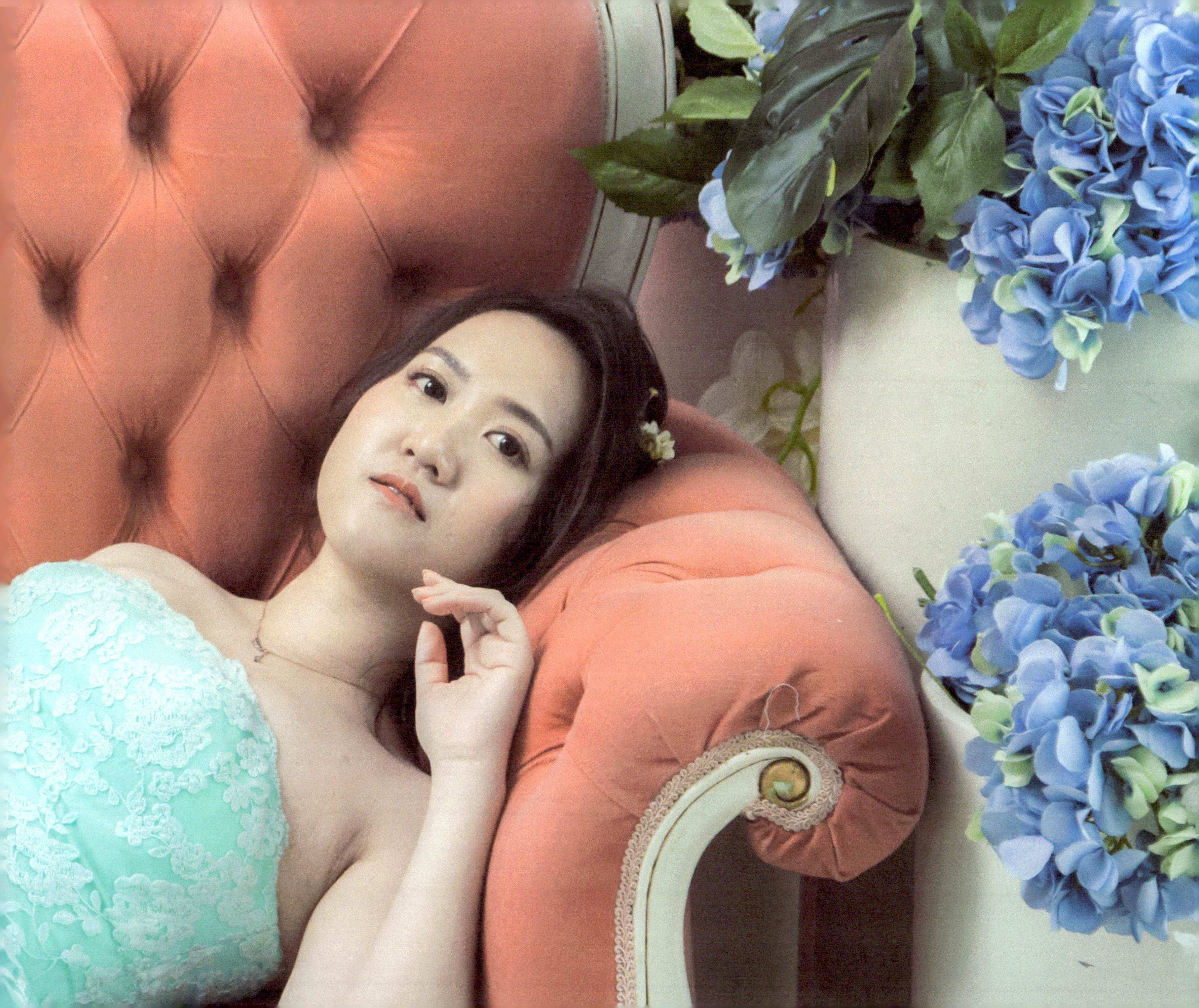

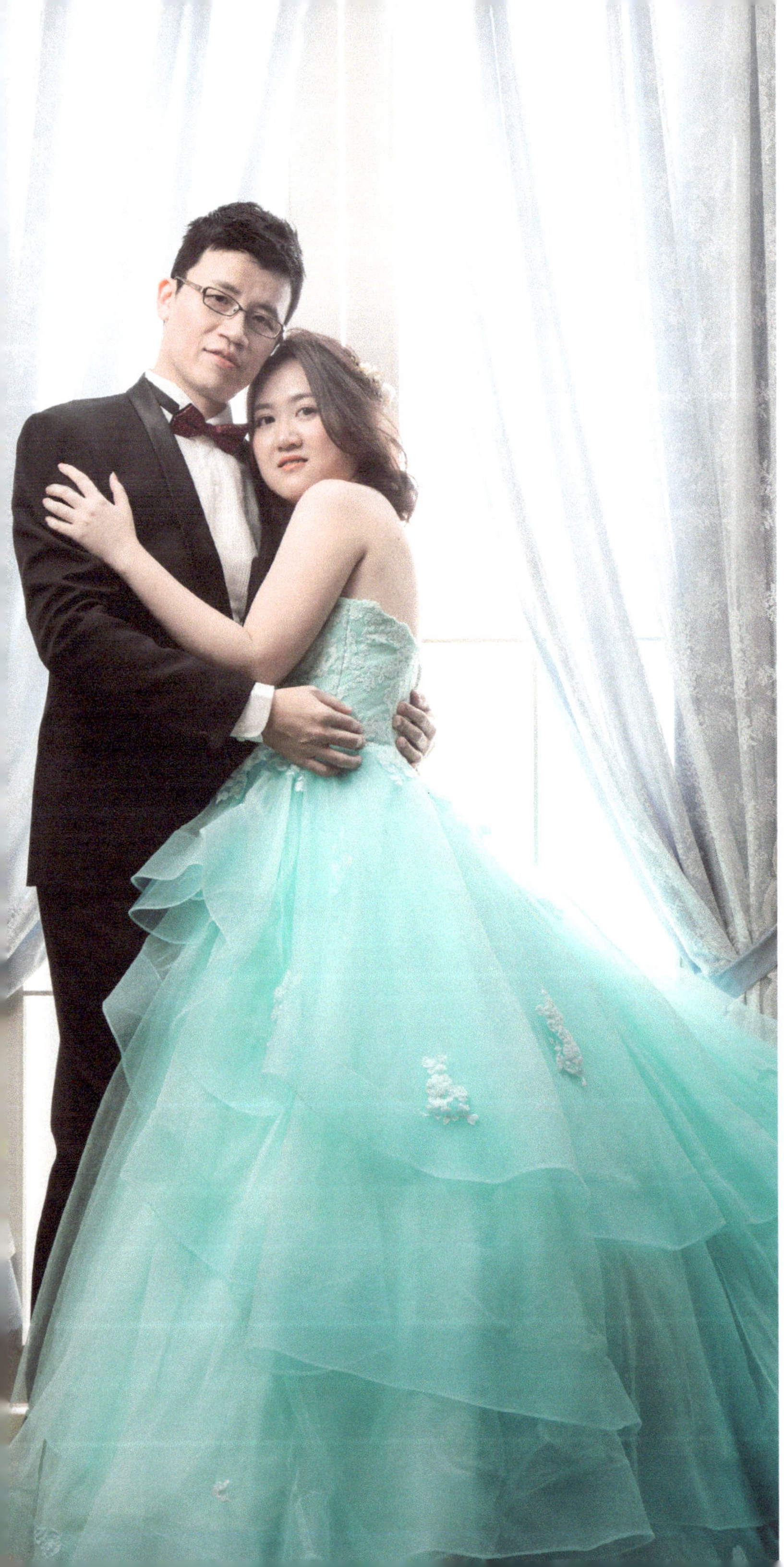
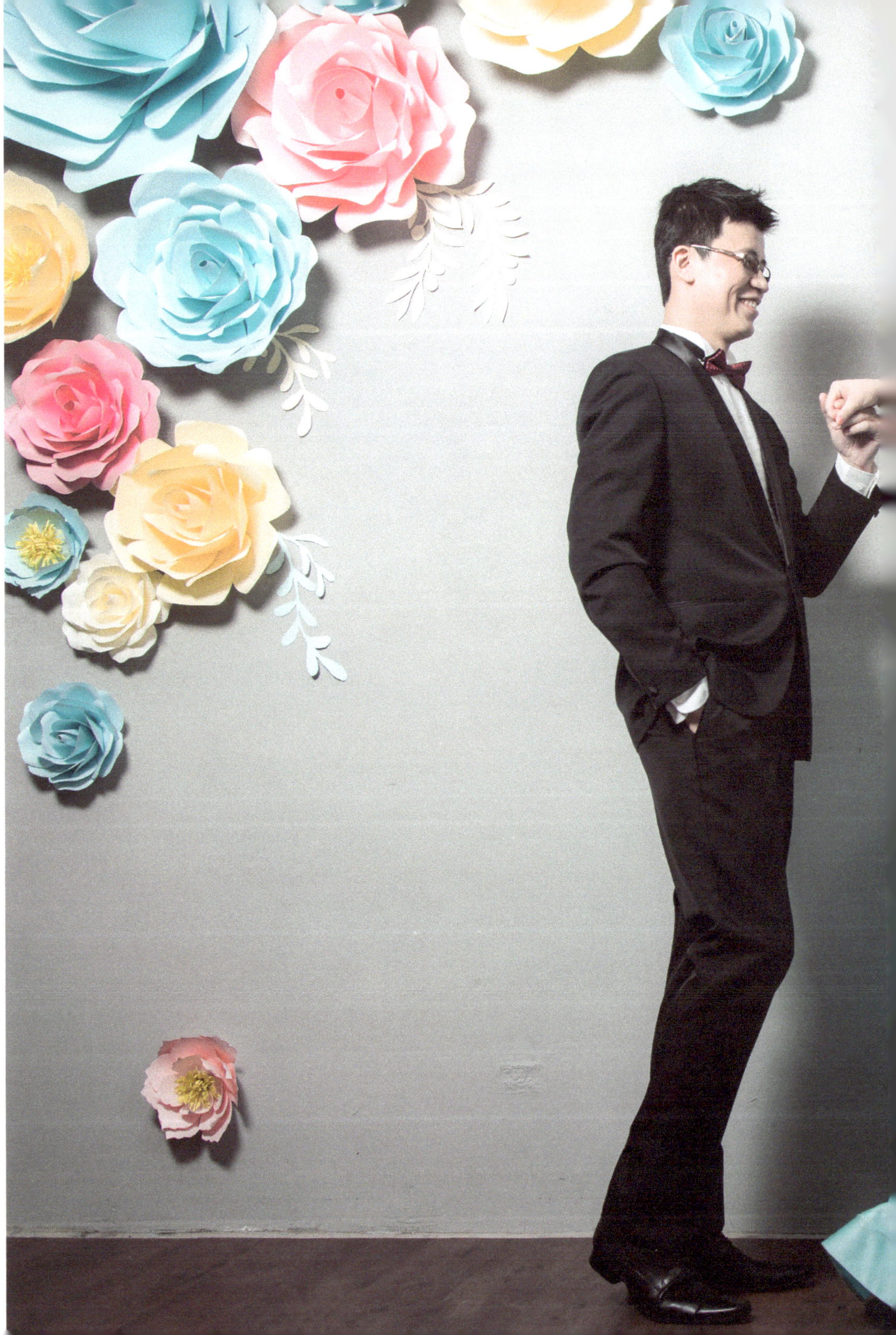

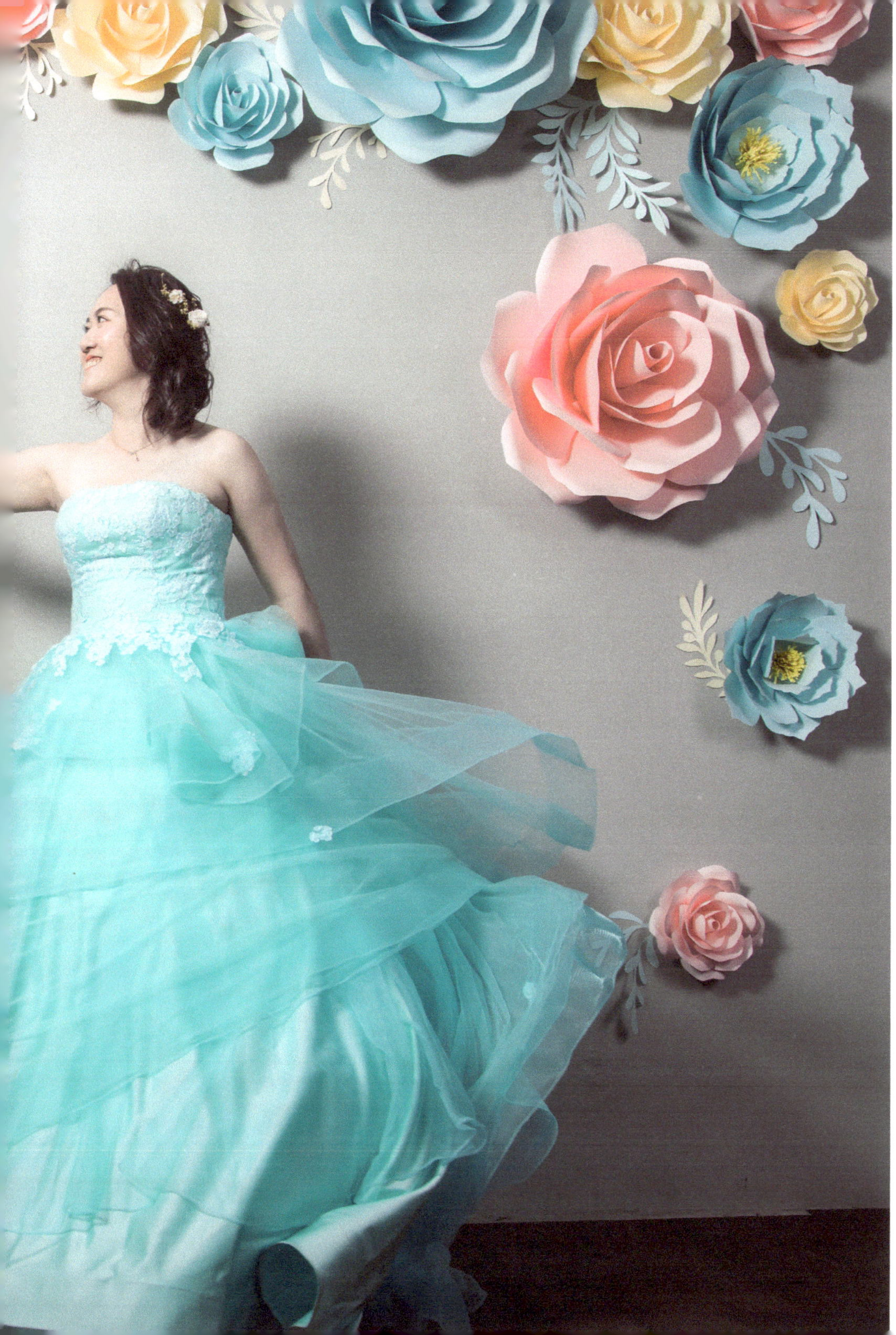

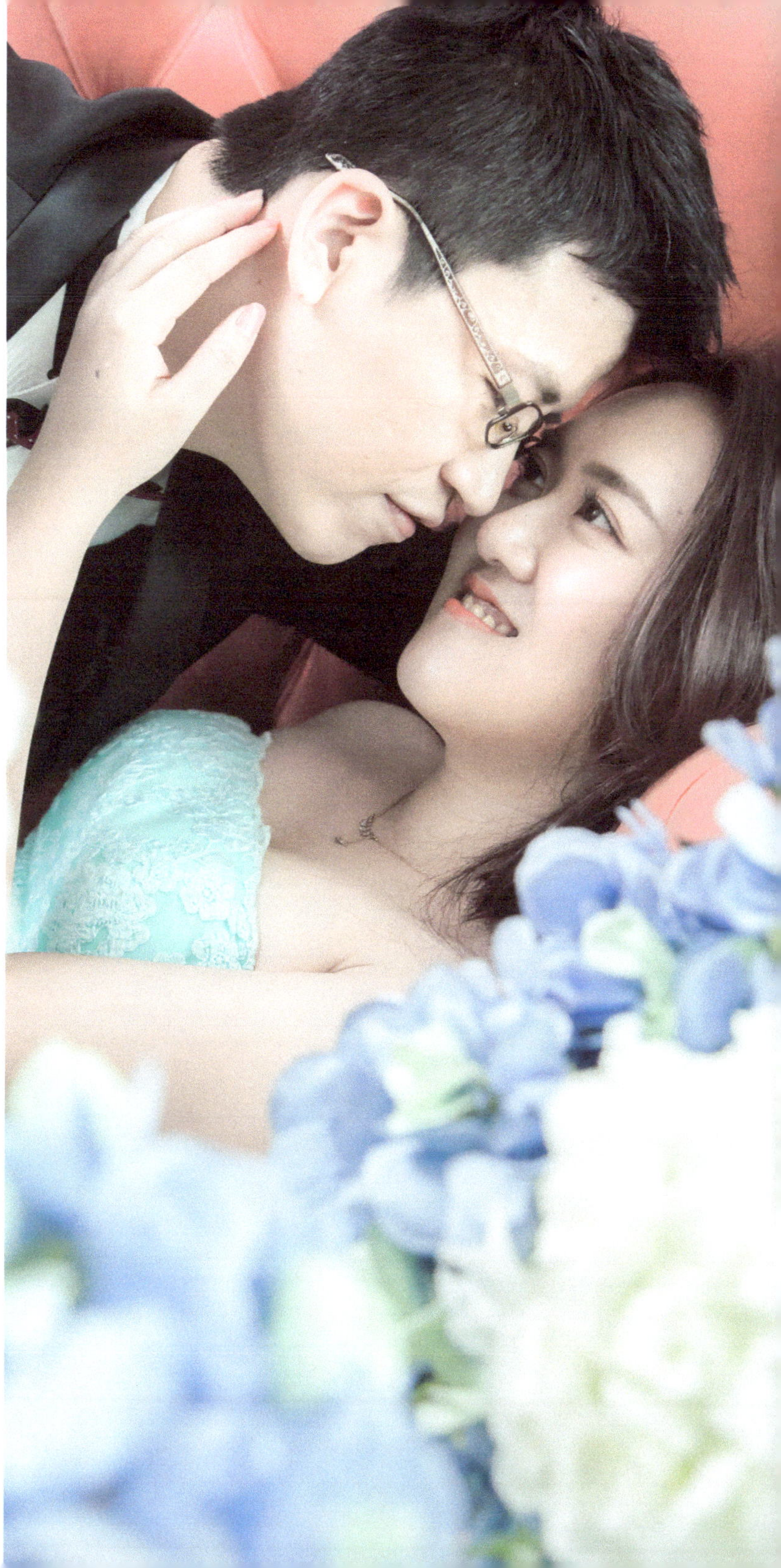

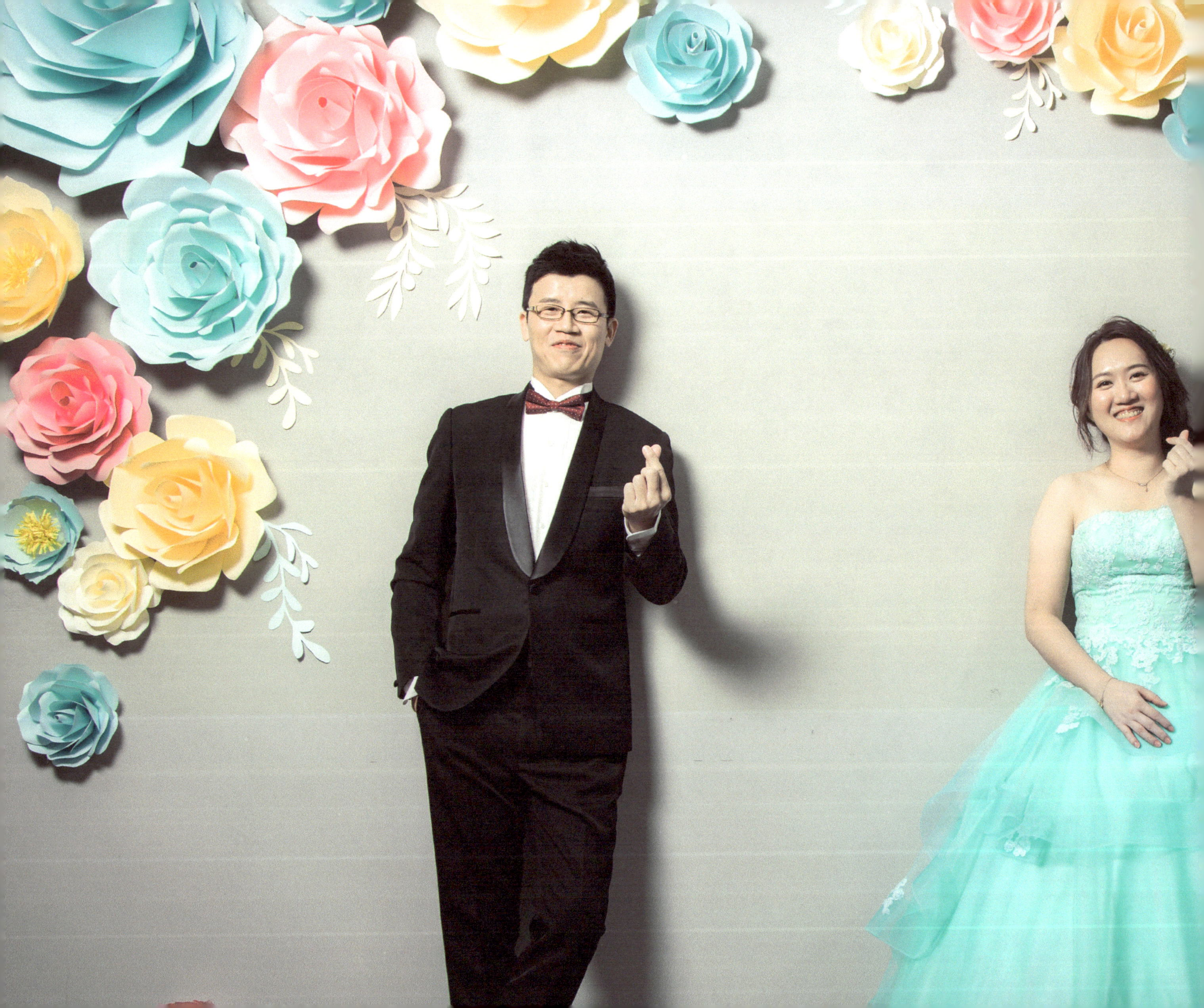

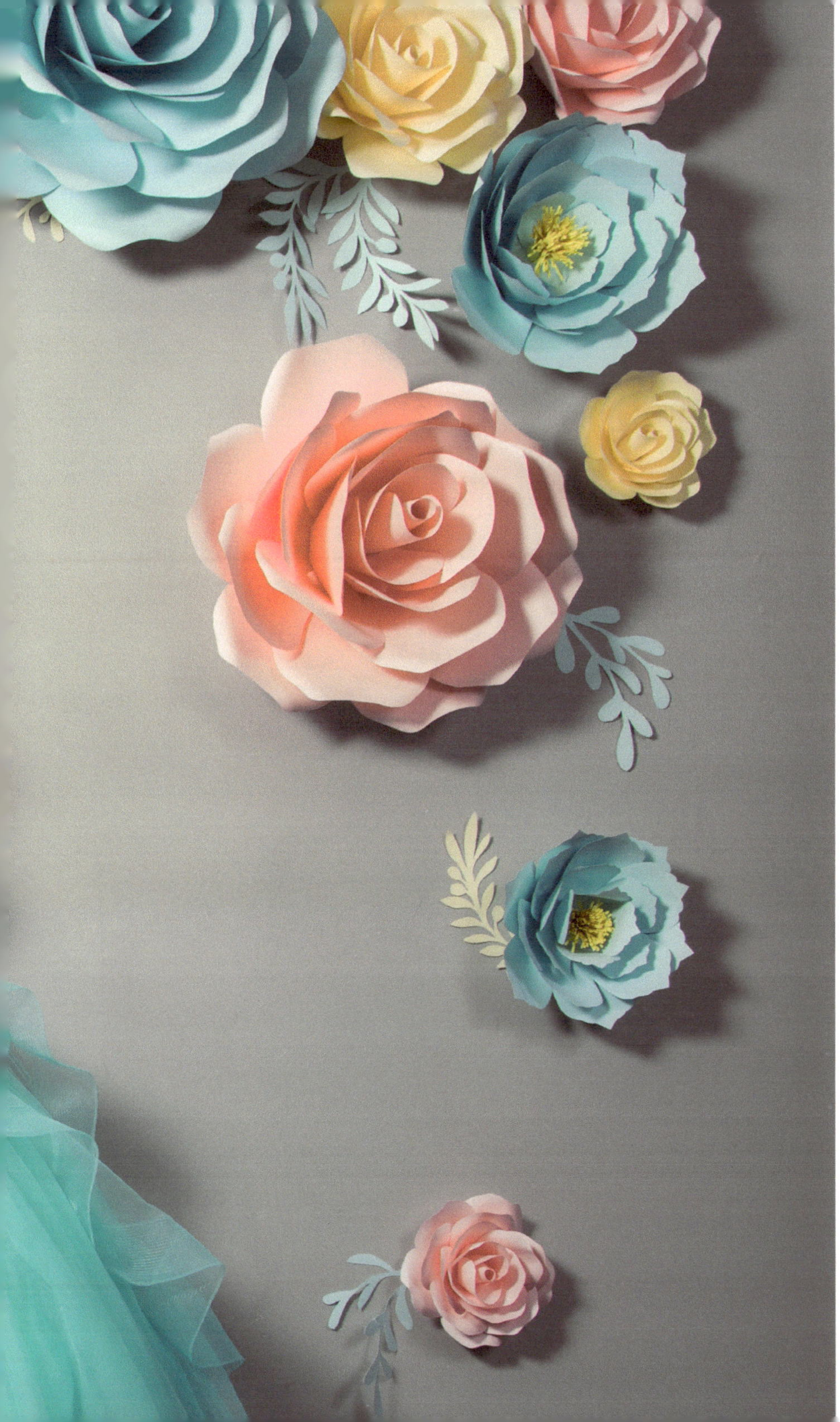
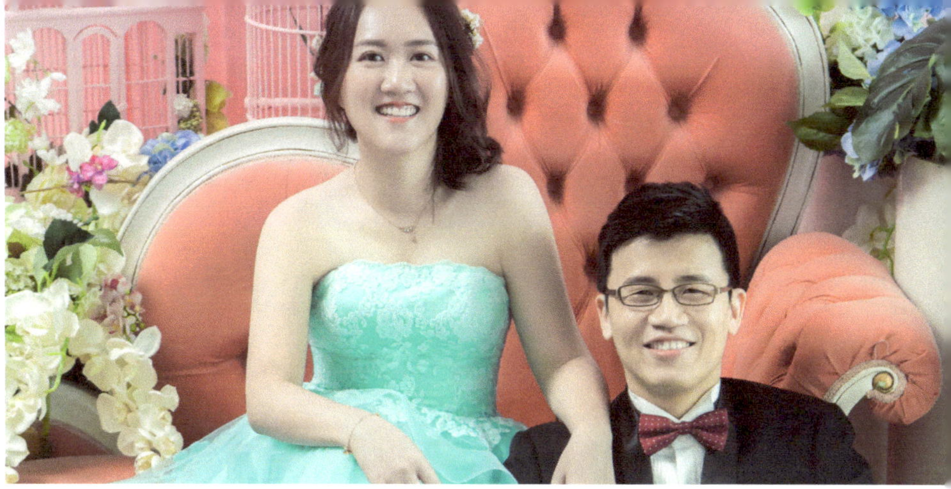
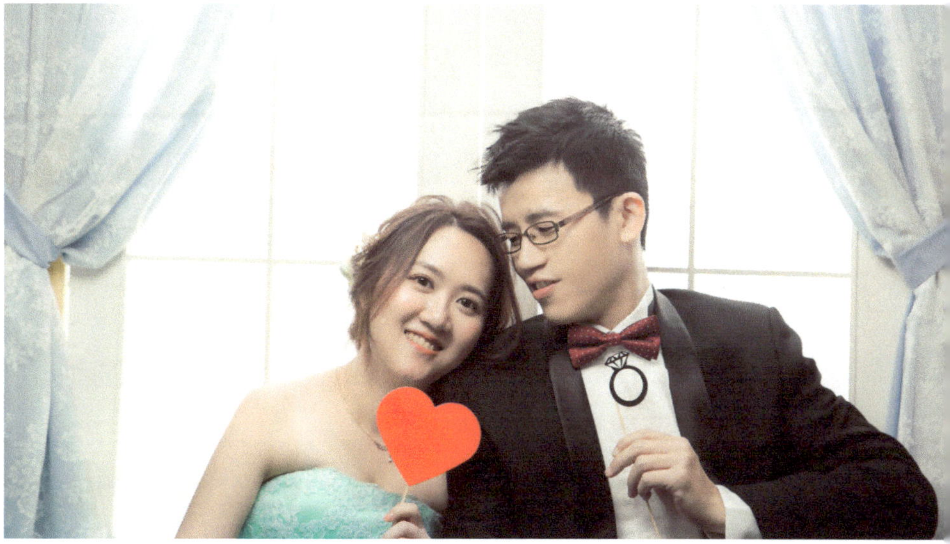
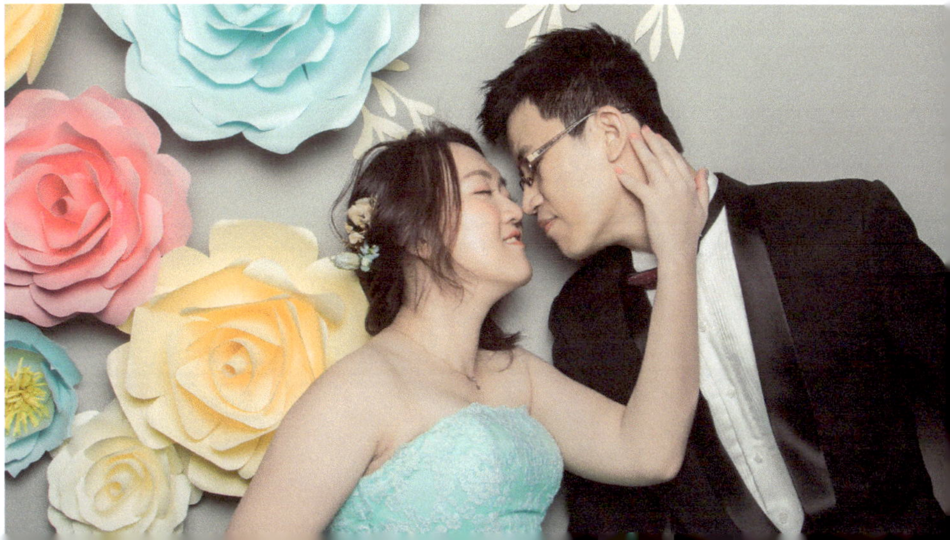

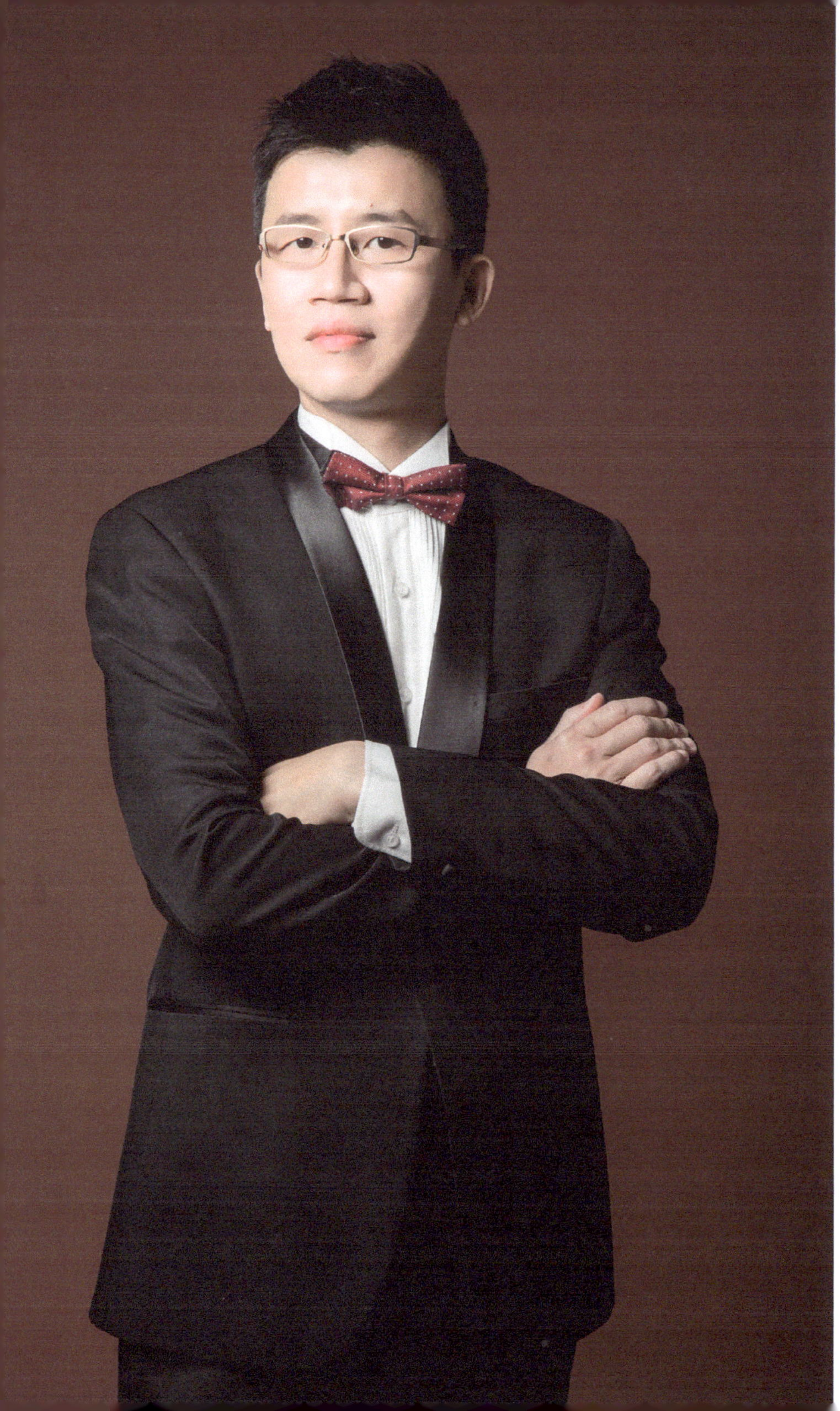
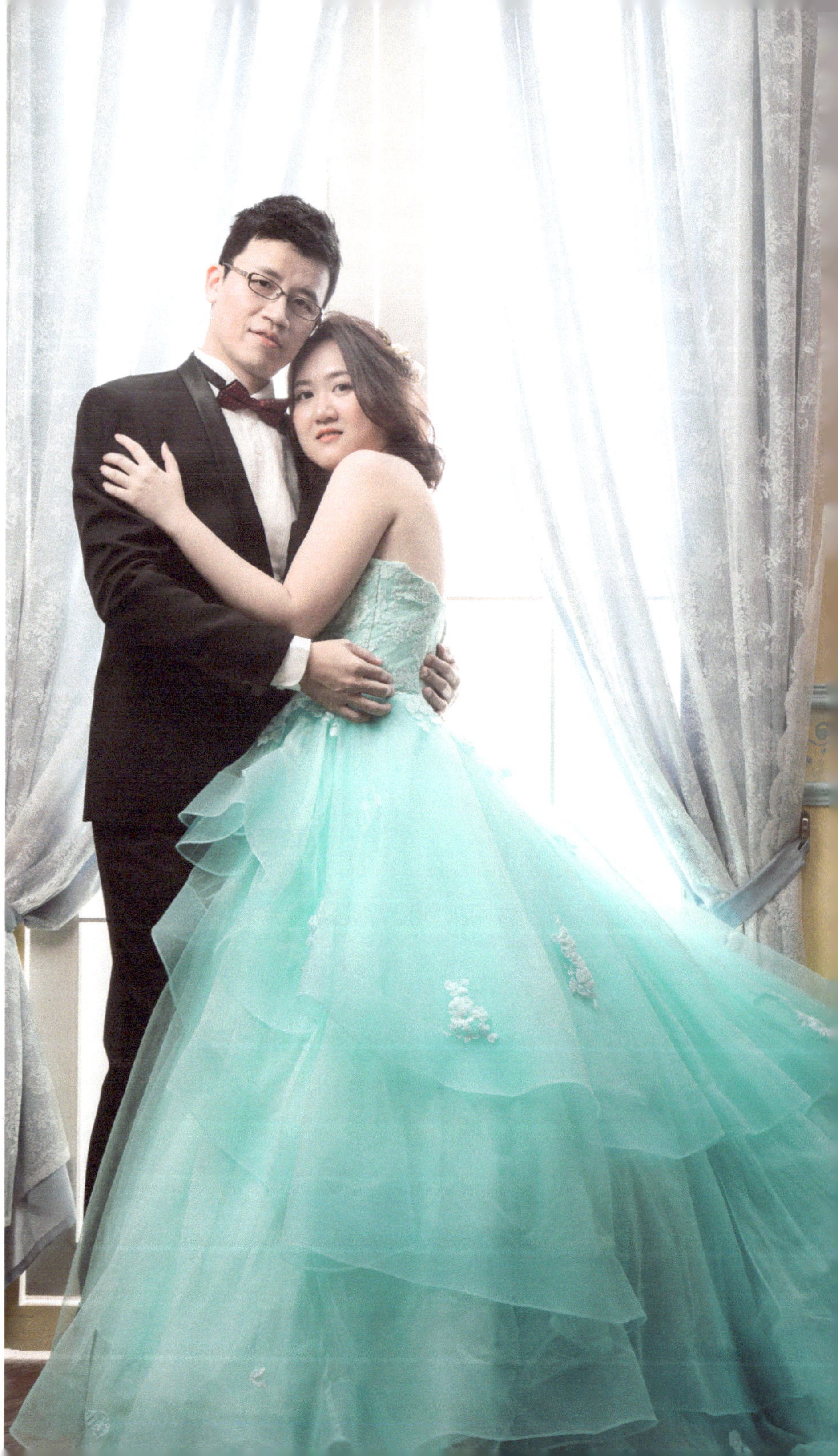

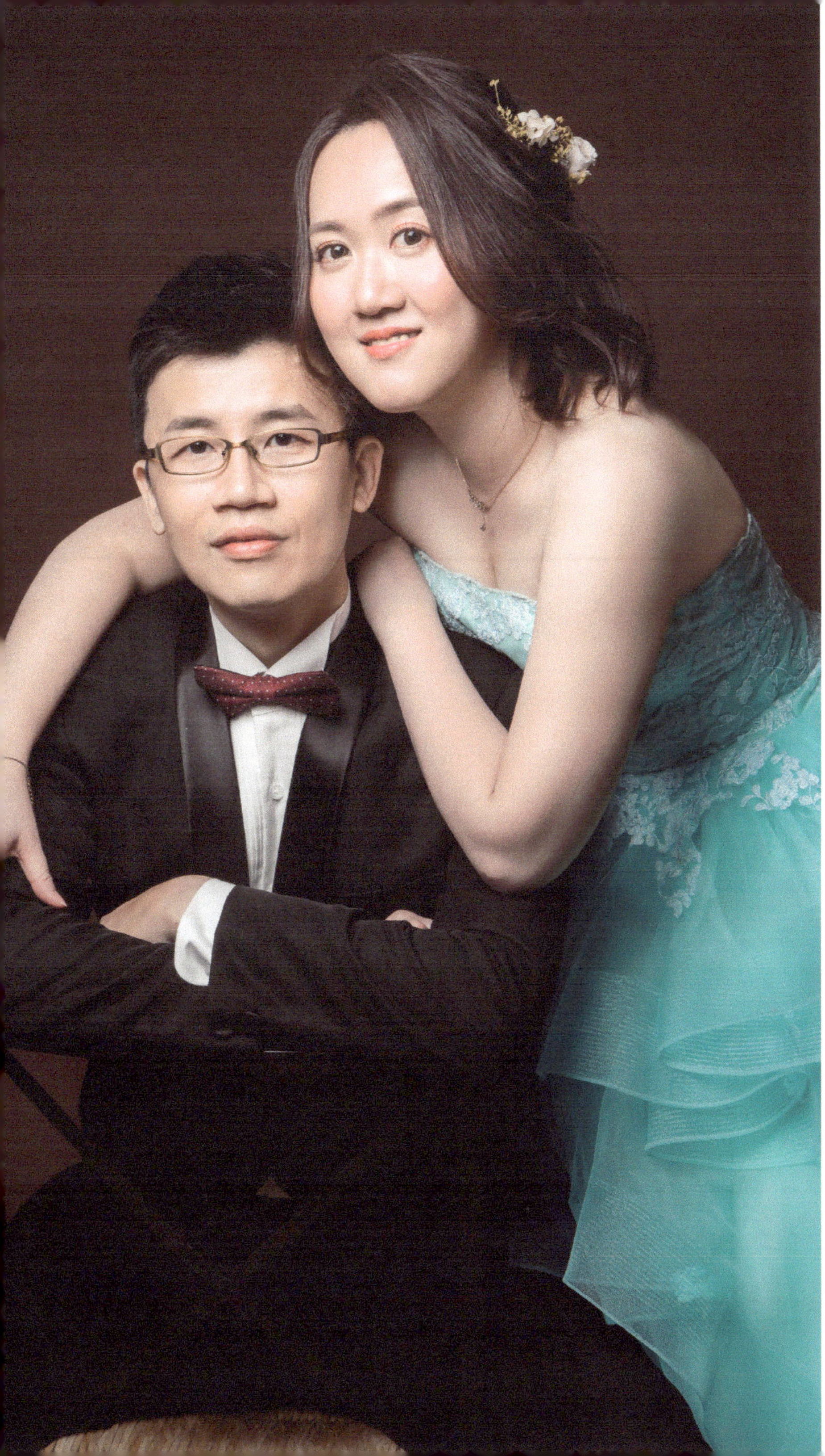
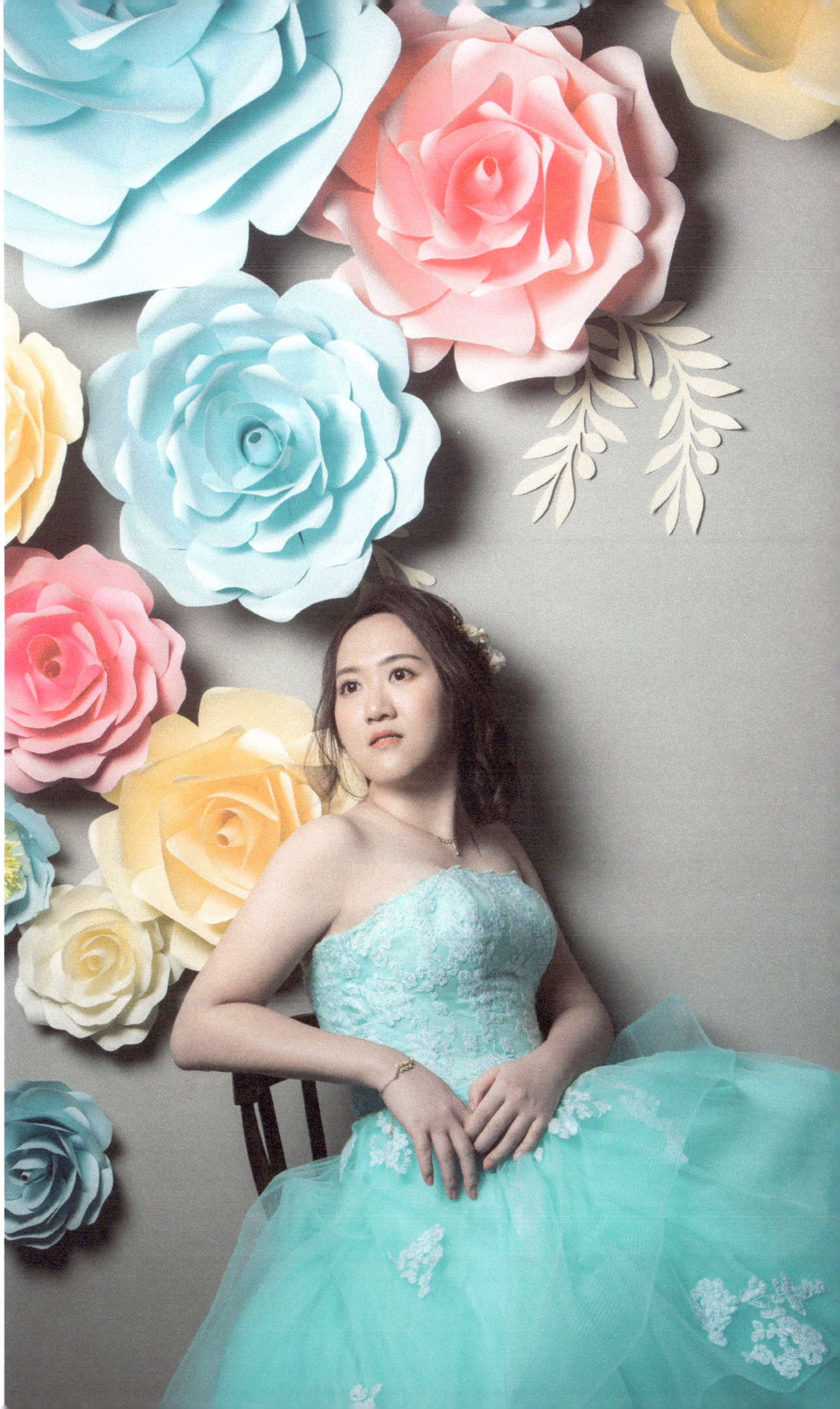

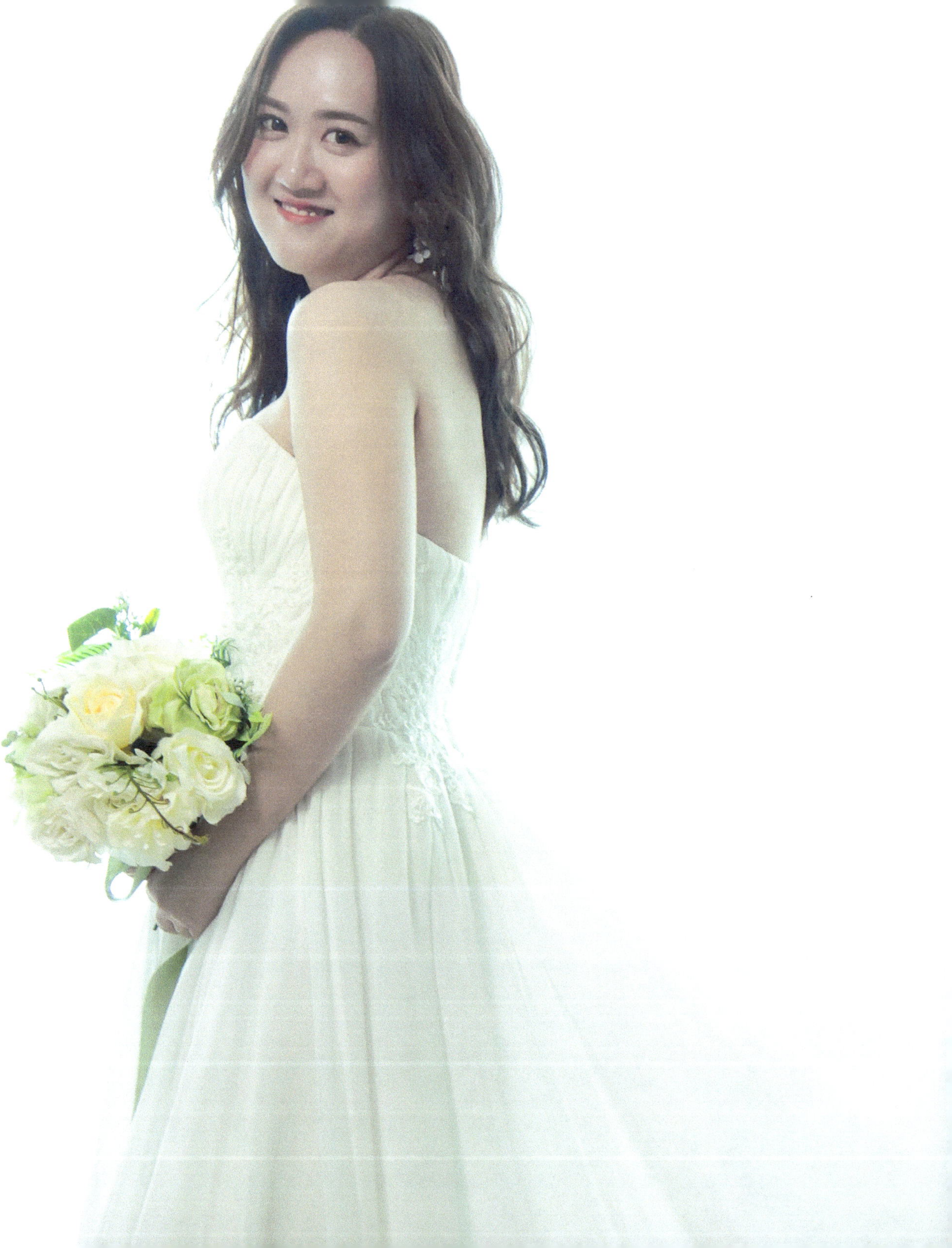

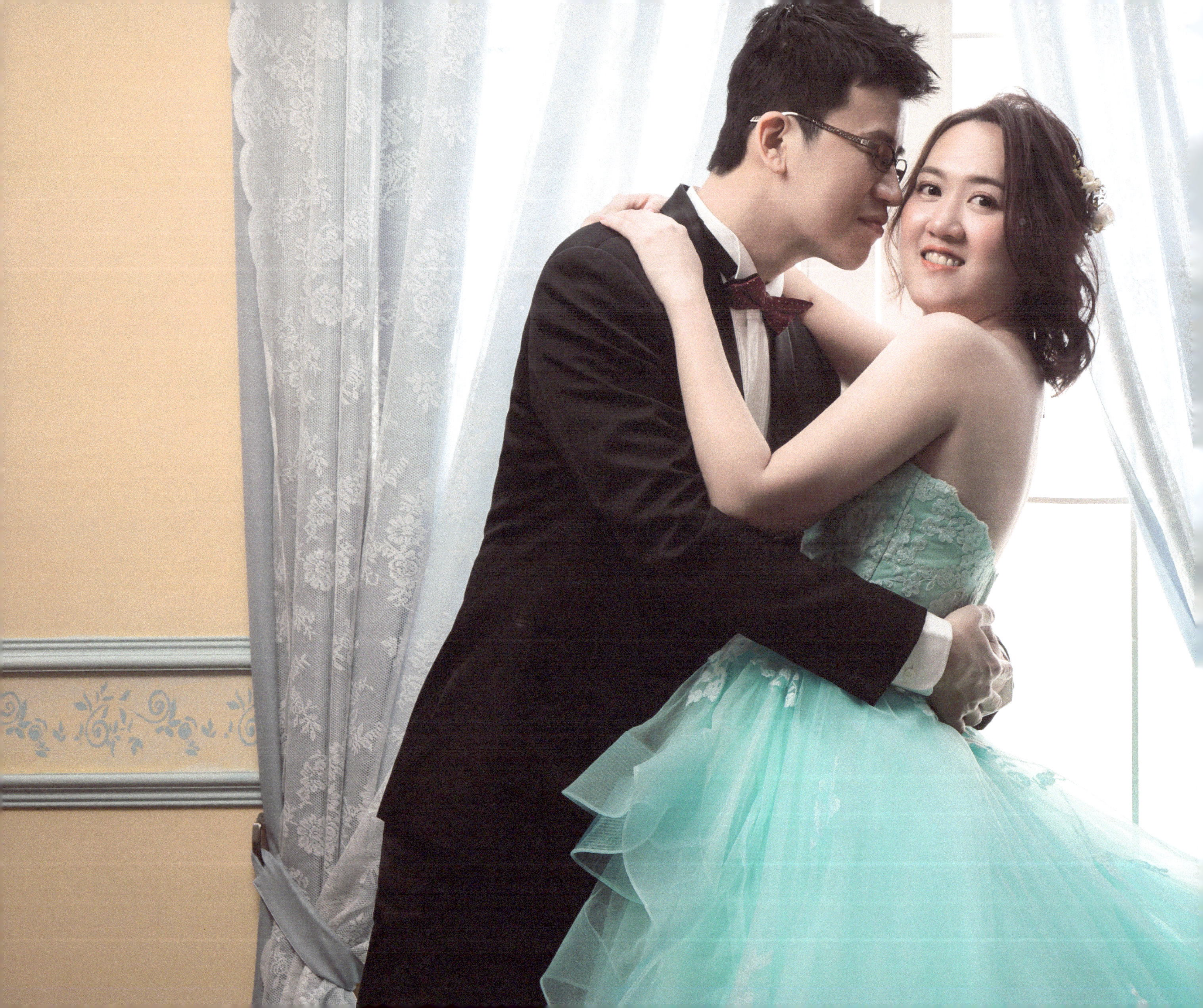

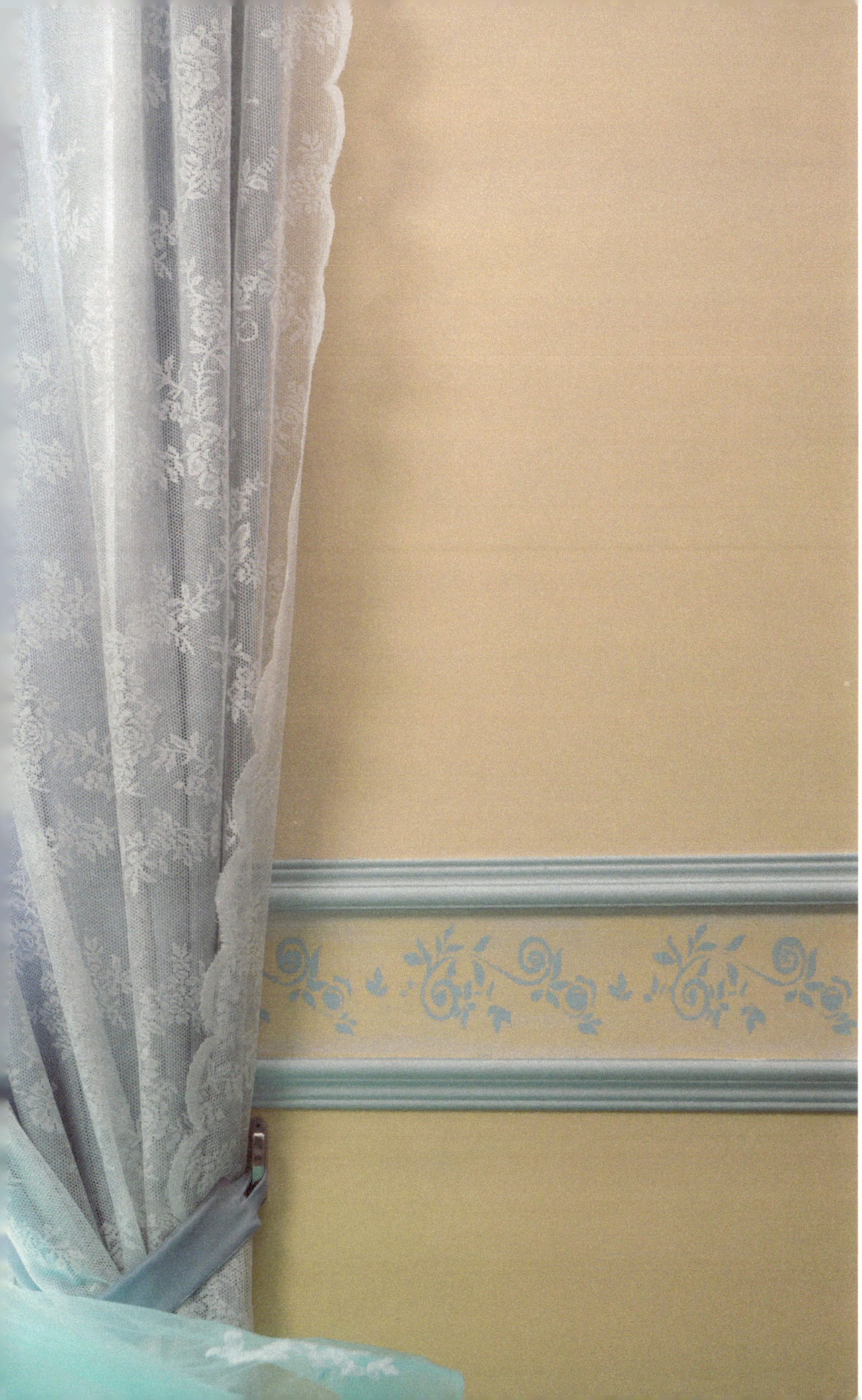
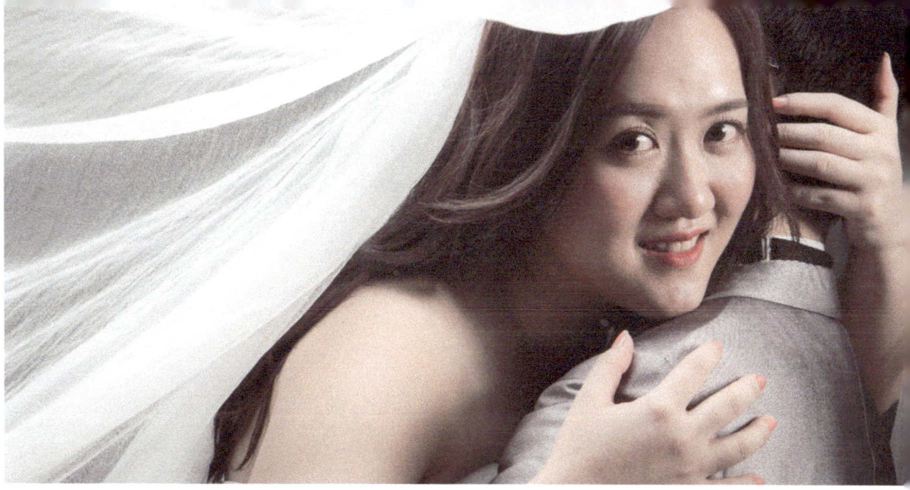
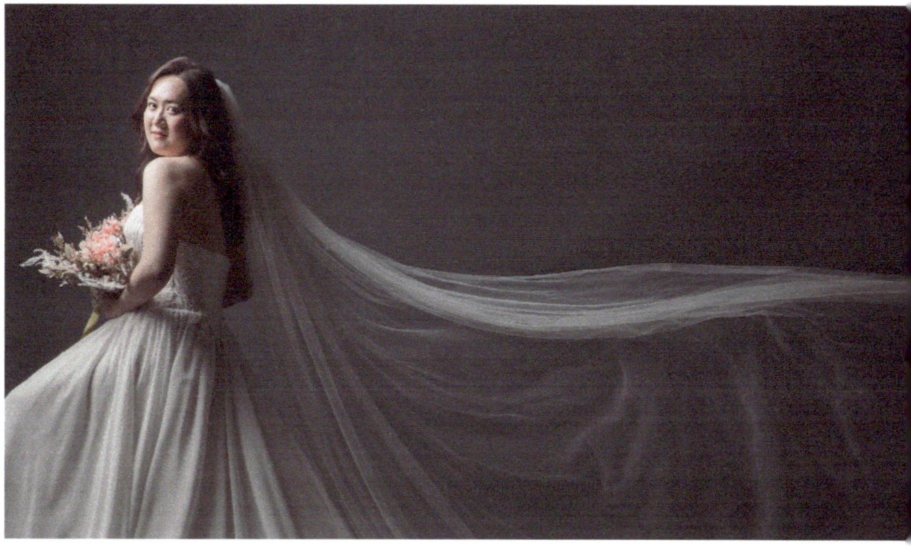
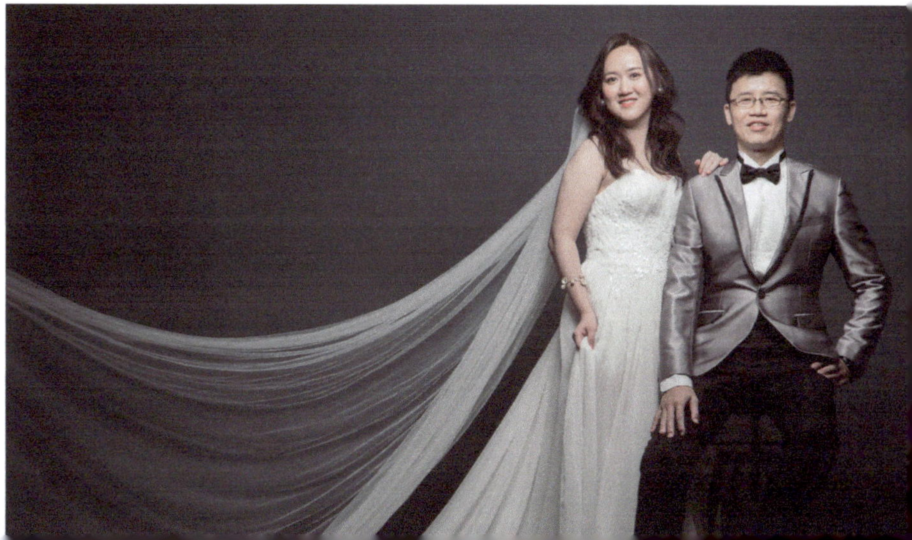

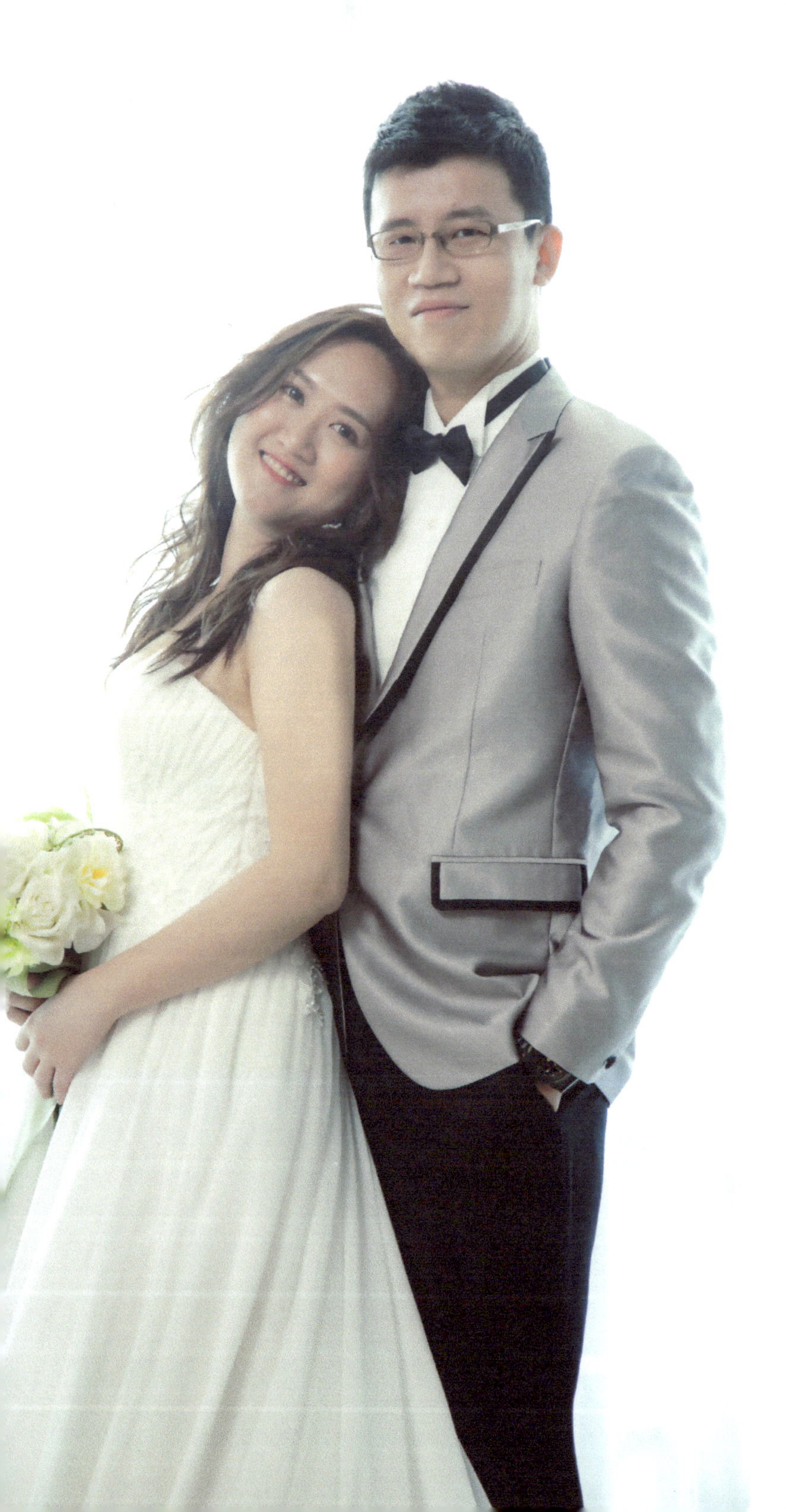
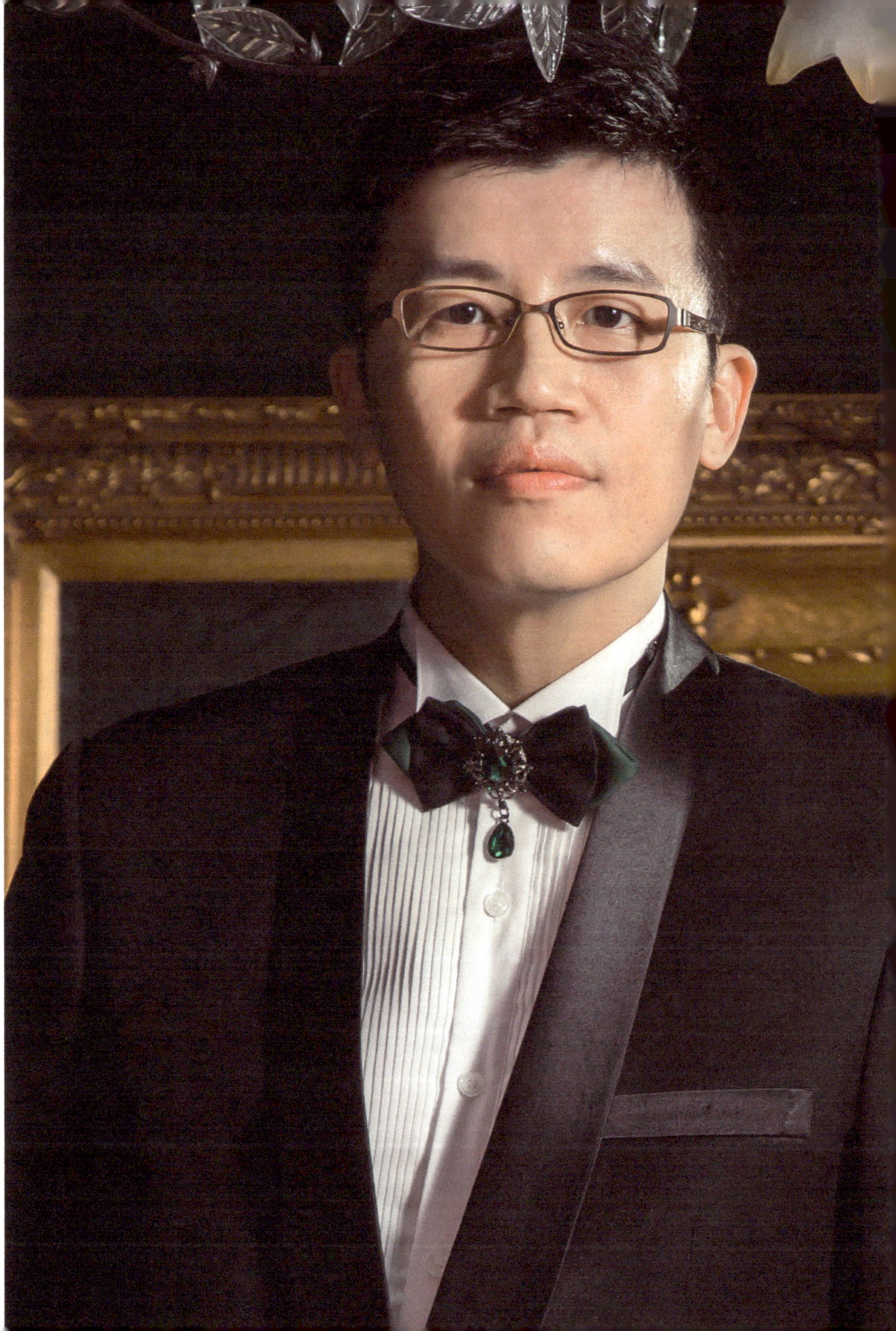

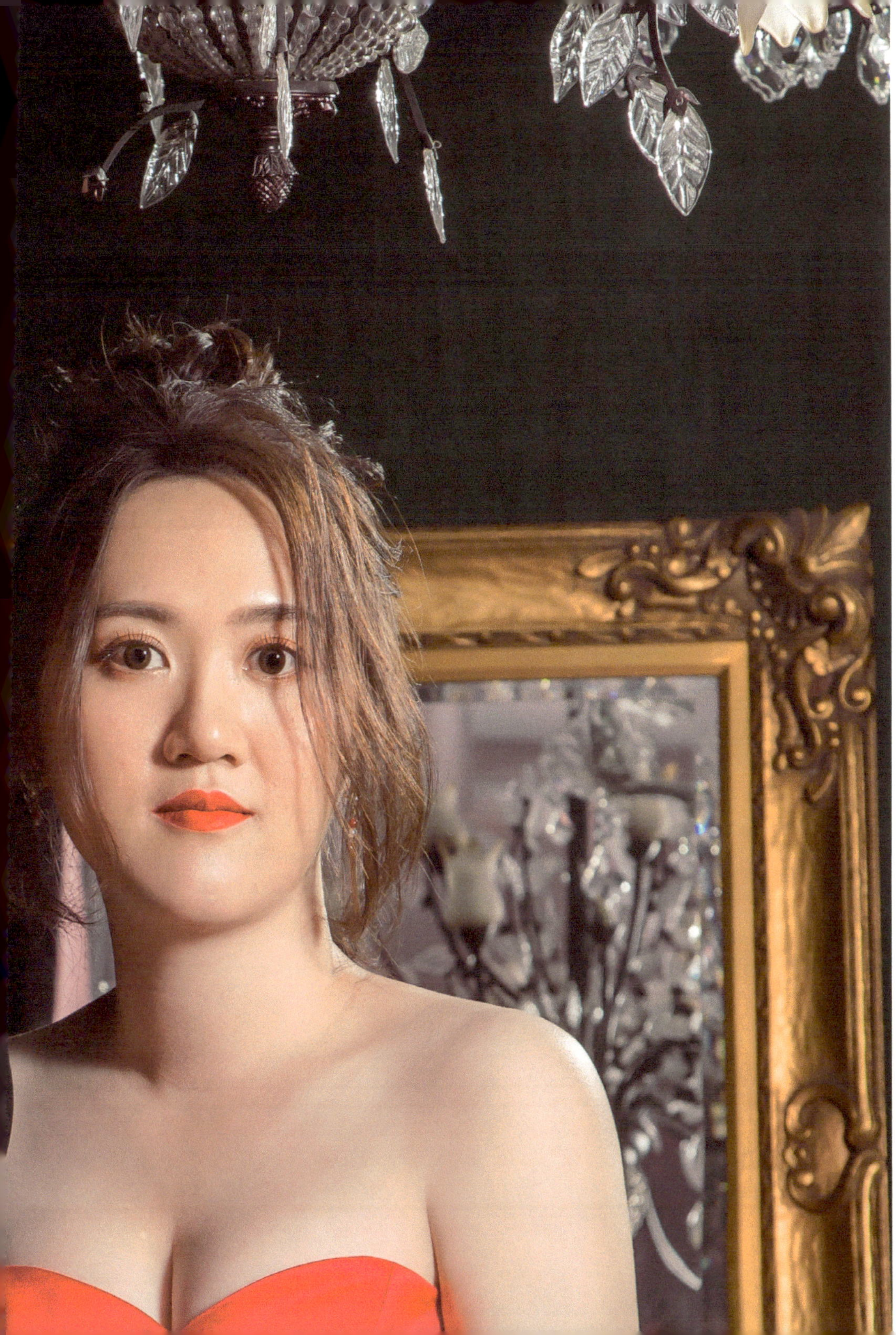
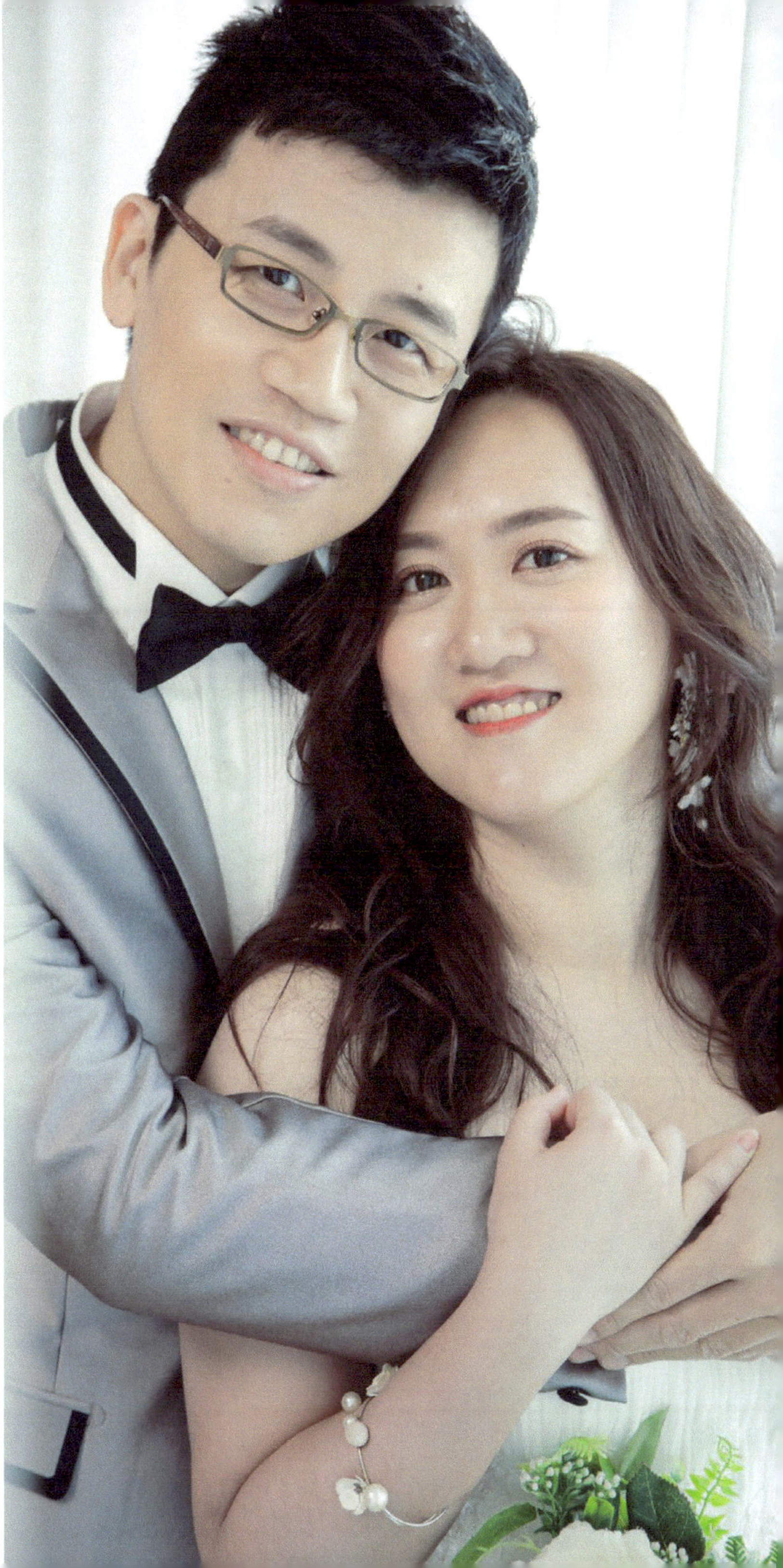

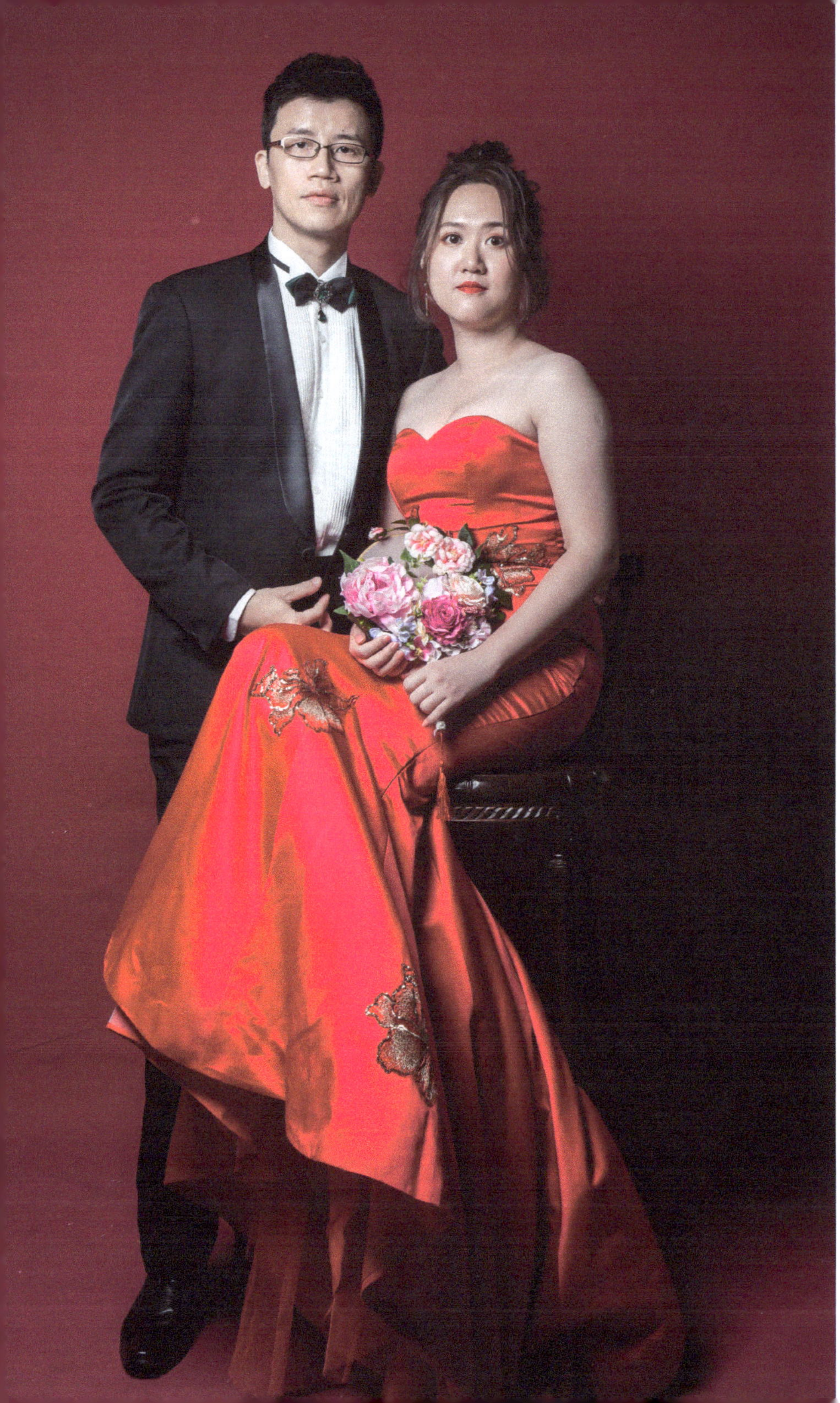
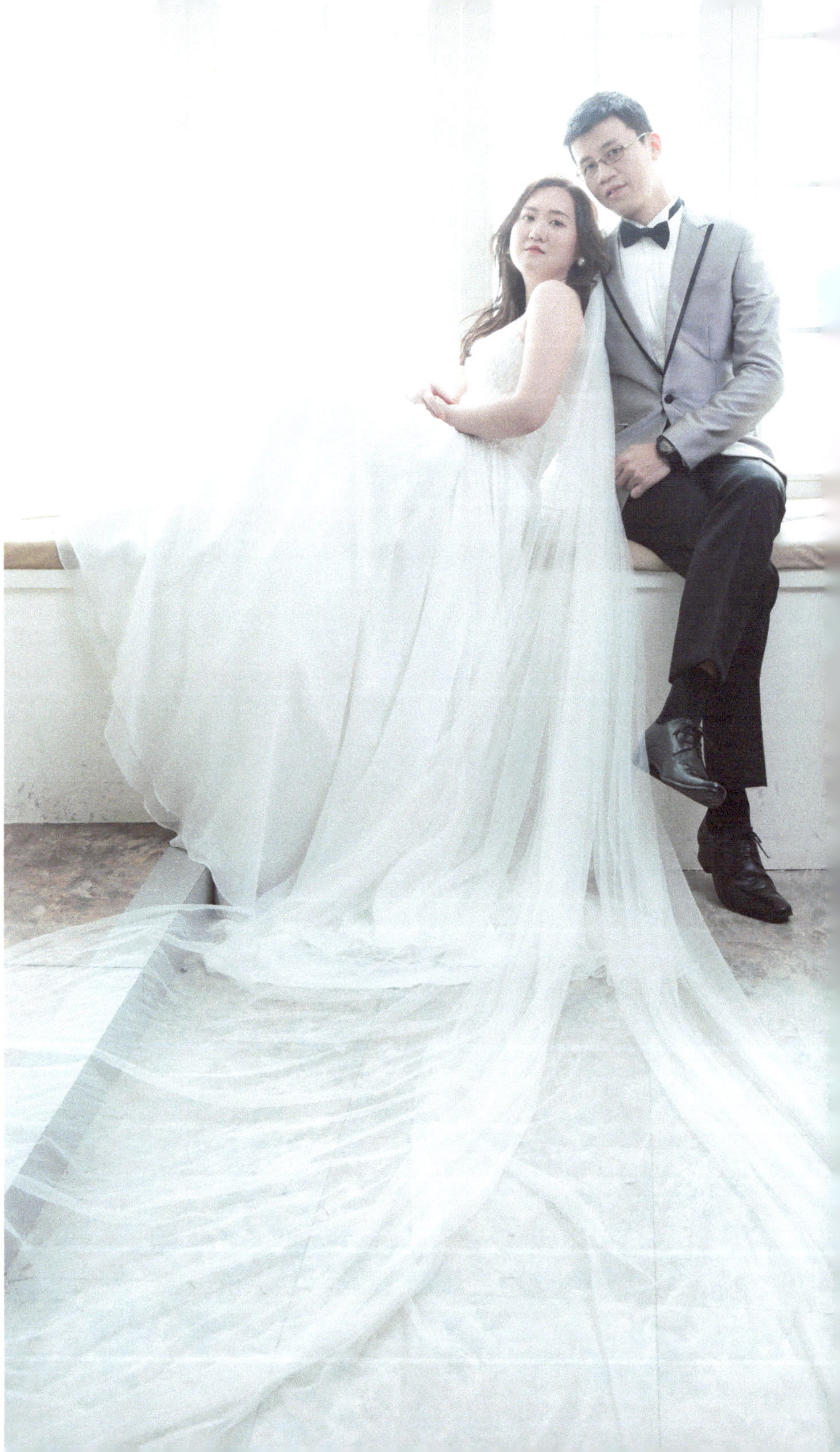

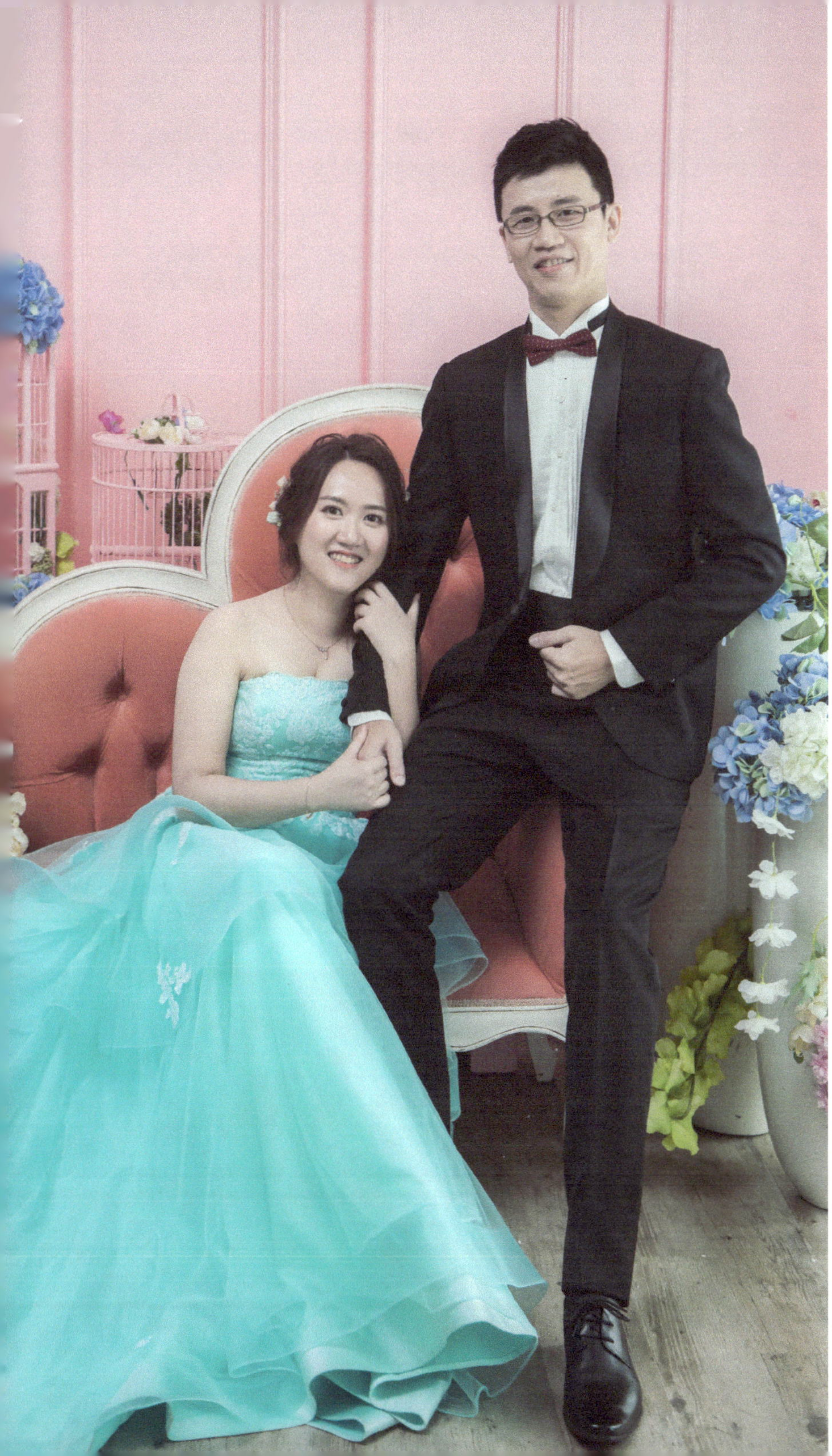

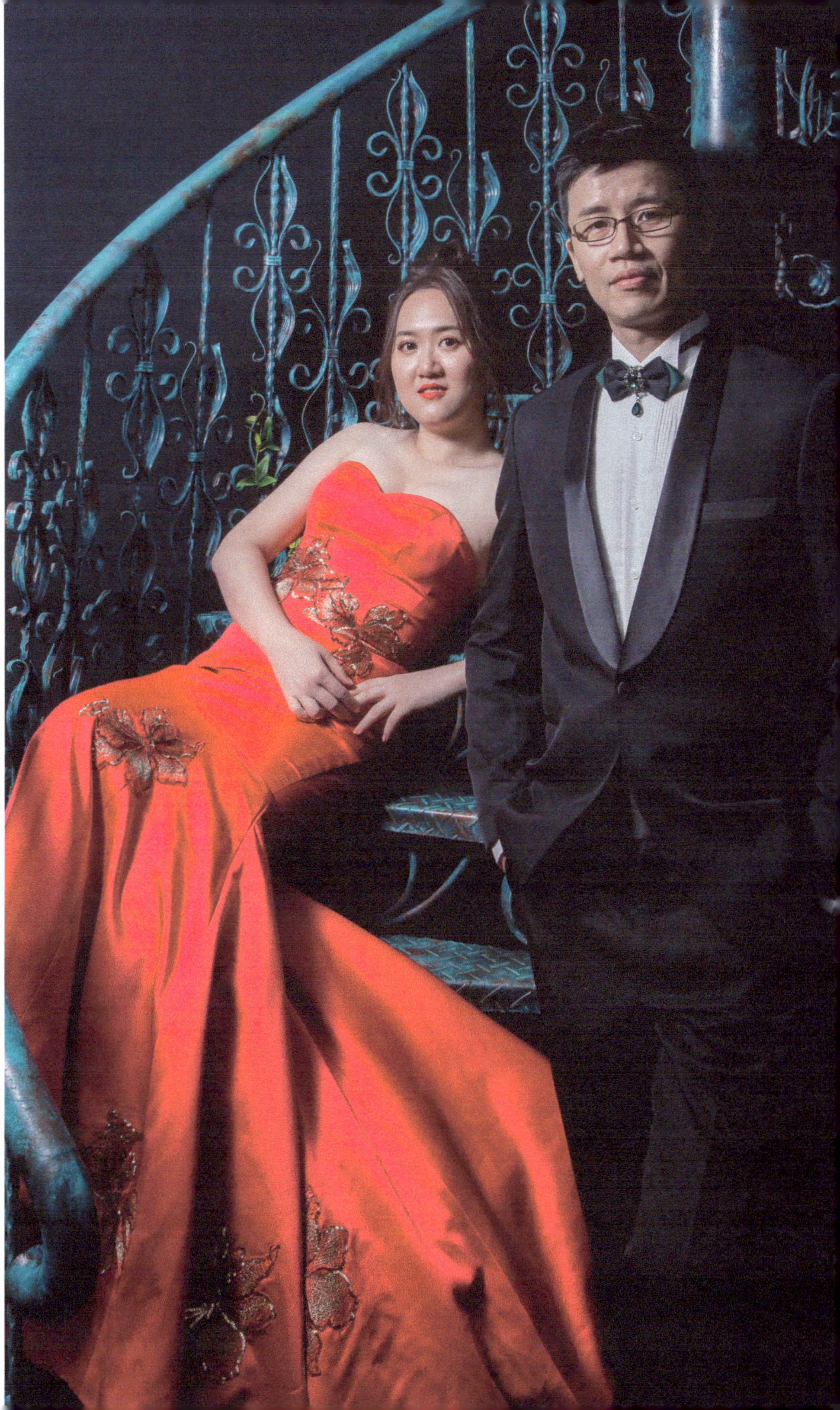

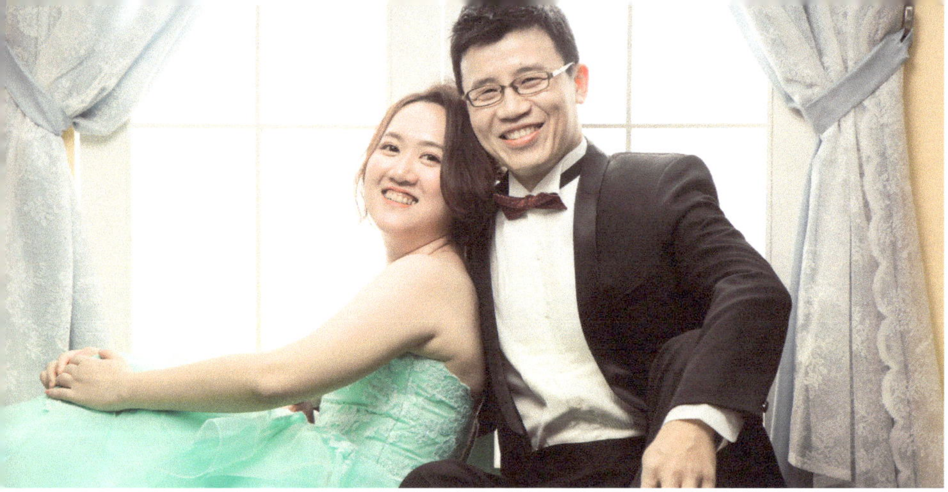
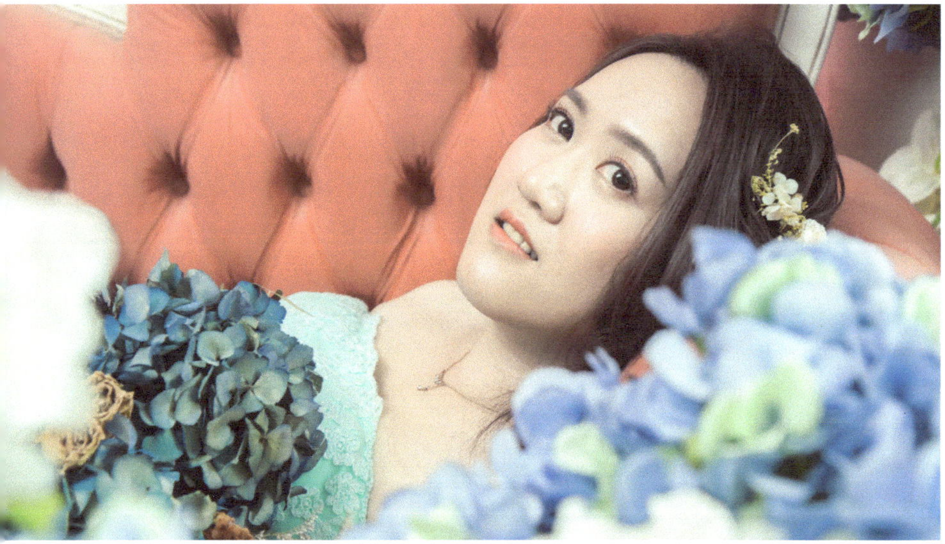
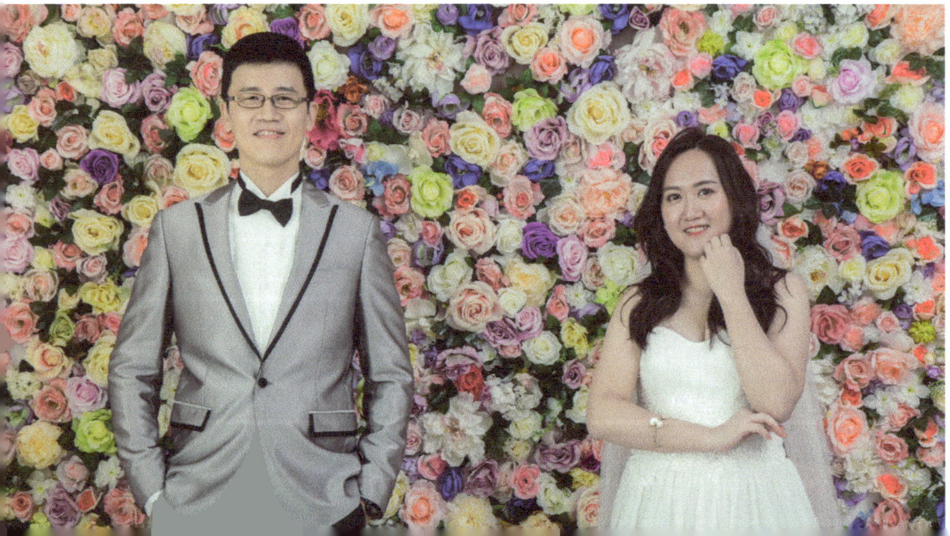
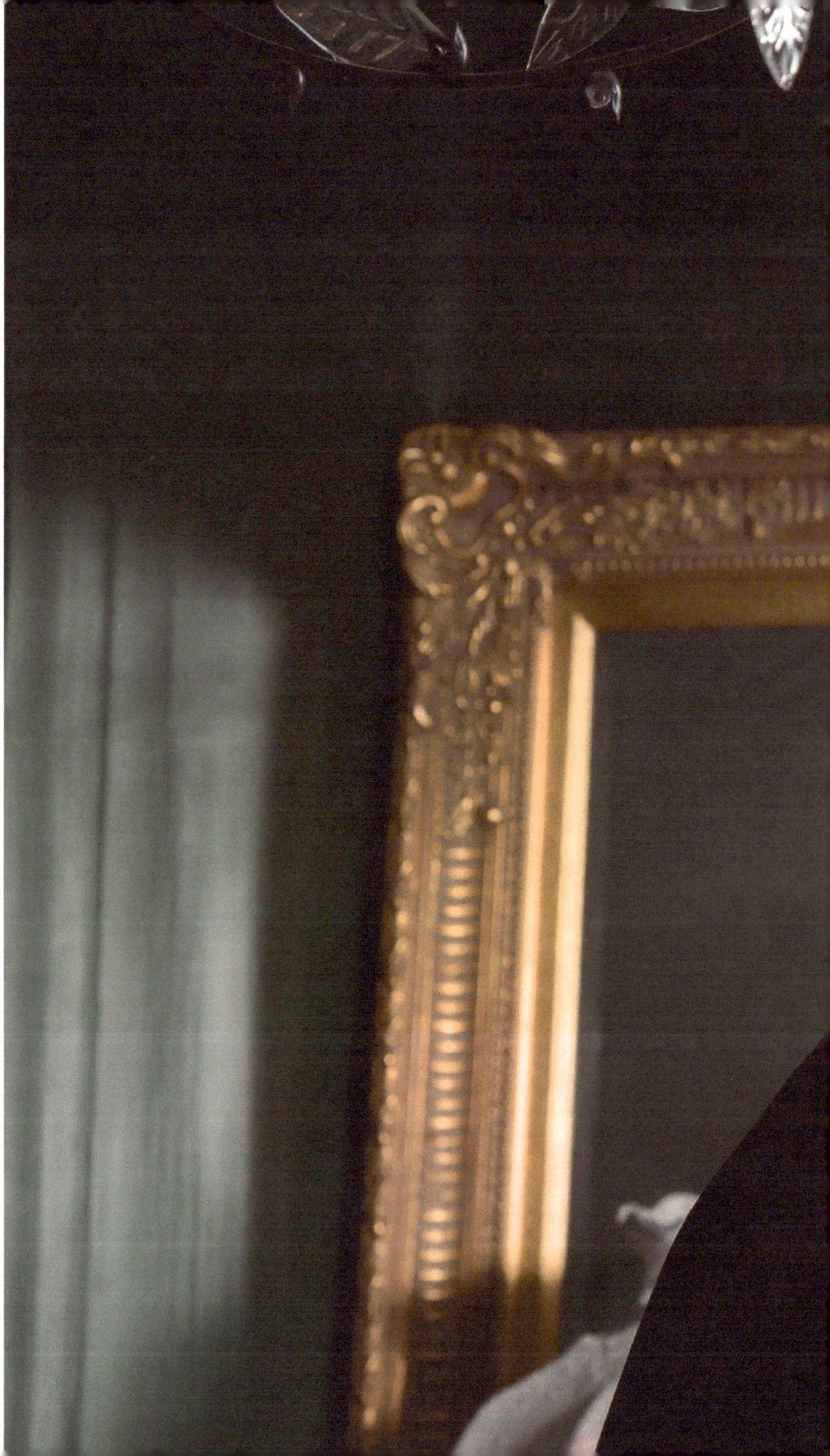

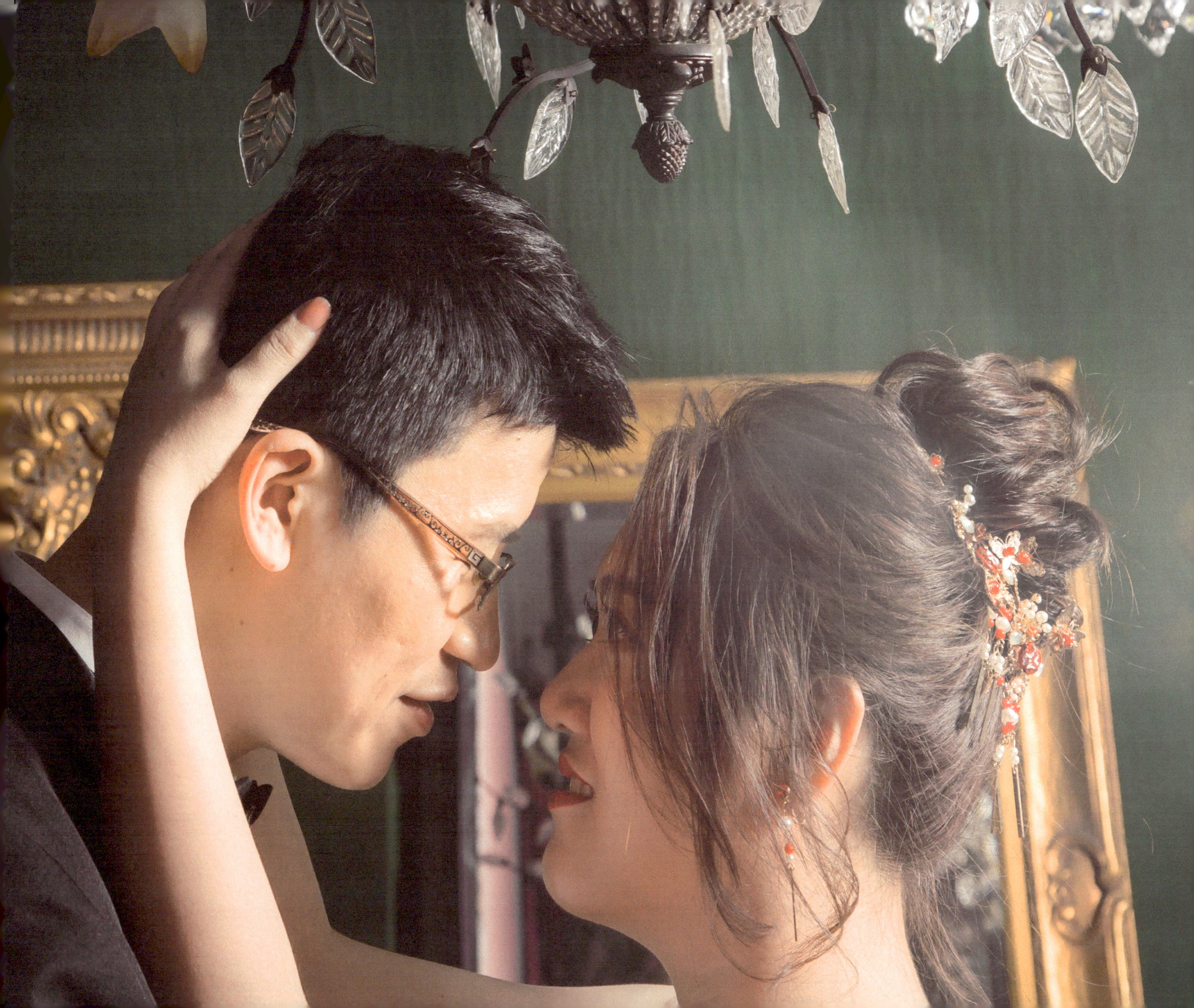

www.ingramcontent.com/pod-product-compliance
Lightning Source LLC
Chambersburg PA
CBHW040804300326
41914CB00064B/1603
9780578636405